# Victory Has a Thousand Fathers

## Sources of Success in Counterinsurgency

T0306857

Christopher Paul • Colin P. Clarke • Beth Grill

Prepared for the Office of the Secretary of Defense

Approved for public release; distribution unlimited

RAND NATIONAL DEFENSE RESEARCH INSTITUTE

The research described in this report was prepared for the Office of the Secretary of Defense (OSD). The research was conducted in the RAND National Defense Research Institute, a federally funded research and development center sponsored by OSD, the Joint Staff, the Unified Combatant Commands, the Department of the Navy, the Marine Corps, the defense agencies, and the defense Intelligence Community under Contract W74V8H-06-C-0002.

**Library of Congress Control Number: 2010930813**

ISBN: 978-0-8330-4961-2

The RAND Corporation is a nonprofit research organization providing objective analysis and effective solutions that address the challenges facing the public and private sectors around the world. RAND's publications do not necessarily reflect the opinions of its research clients and sponsors.
**RAND®** is a registered trademark.

*Cover photo: A U.S. marine stands in a doorway after searching one of the houses of Saddam Hussein's family in Owja, Iraq, April 15, 2003. The village, which is just outside Tikrit, was the former leader's birthplace. AP Photo/Kevin Frayer.*

© Copyright 2010 RAND Corporation

Permission is given to duplicate this document for personal use only, as long as it is unaltered and complete. Copies may not be duplicated for commercial purposes. Unauthorized posting of RAND documents to a non-RAND website is prohibited. RAND documents are protected under copyright law. For information on reprint and linking permissions, please visit the RAND permissions page (http://www.rand.org/publications/permissions.html).

Published 2010 by the RAND Corporation
1776 Main Street, P.O. Box 2138, Santa Monica, CA 90407-2138
1200 South Hayes Street, Arlington, VA 22202-5050
4570 Fifth Avenue, Suite 600, Pittsburgh, PA 15213-2665
RAND URL: http://www.rand.org/
To order RAND documents or to obtain additional information, contact
Distribution Services: Telephone: (310) 451-7002;
Fax: (310) 451-6915; Email: order@rand.org

# Preface

This research grew out of the sponsor's desire to be able to evidence the historical contribution (or lack of contribution) of activities concordant with what is now referred to as *strategic communication* to the outcomes of counterinsurgency (COIN) campaigns. The method that the RAND Corporation proposed to answer this question—a combination of historical case studies and the qualitative comparative approach—was capable of answering a much broader set of questions about the contributions of a wider range of approaches to COIN with minimal additional effort. This research, then, reports on the demonstrated effectiveness of a variety of approaches to COIN (including strategic communication) through case studies of the world's 30 most recent resolved insurgencies.

This monograph describes the qualitative comparative approach, presents findings from the overall analyses, and explains the study's case selection and methodology. It also presents an overview and in-depth assessments of the key approaches, practices, and factors that feature prominently in successful COIN operations. A companion volume, *Victory Has a Thousand Fathers: Detailed Counterinsurgency Case Studies*, includes detailed case histories for each of the COIN campaigns examined in the analyses.[1] The full case data can be downloaded at http://www.rand.org/pubs/monographs/MG964/.

---

[1] Christopher Paul, Colin P. Clarke, and Beth Grill, *Victory Has a Thousand Fathers: Detailed Counterinsurgency Case Studies*, Santa Monica, Calif.: RAND Corporation, MG-964/1-OSD, 2010.

This work will be of interest to defense analysts and military planners who are responsible for evaluating current U.S. operations and COIN approaches; to academics and scholars who engage in historical research of COIN, insurgency, and irregular warfare; and to students of contemporary and historic international conflicts.

This research was sponsored by the Office of the Secretary of Defense, Cost Analysis and Program Evaluation, Irregular Warfare Division (OSD[CAPE]IW), and conducted within the International Security and Defense Policy Center of the RAND National Defense Research Institute, a federally funded research and development center sponsored by the Office of the Secretary of Defense, the Joint Staff, the Unified Combatant Commands, the Navy, the Marine Corps, the defense agencies, and the defense Intelligence Community.

For more information on RAND's International Security and Defense Policy Center, contact the Director, James Dobbins. He can be reached by email at James_Dobbins@rand.org; by phone at 703-413-1100, extension 5134; or by mail at the RAND Corporation, 1200 South Hayes Street, Arlington, Virginia 22202-5050. More information about RAND is available at www.rand.org.

# Contents

# Figures

# Tables

## Summary

Insurgency has been the most prevalent form of armed conflict since at least 1949.[1] Despite that fact, following the Vietnam War and through the balance of the Cold War, the U.S. military establishment turned its back on insurgency, refusing to consider operations against insurgents as anything other than a "lesser-included case" for forces structured for and prepared to fight two major theater wars. In the post-9/11 world, however, insurgency has rocketed back into prominence. As counterterrorism expert William Rosenau notes, "insurgency and counterinsurgency . . . have enjoyed a level of military, academic, and journalistic notice unseen since the mid-1960s."[2] Countering insurgents, or supporting the efforts of allies and partners as they do so, is the primary focus of ongoing operations in both Iraq and Afghanistan.

When a country becomes host to an insurgency, what counterinsurgency (COIN) approaches give a government the best chance of prevailing? Contemporary discourse on the subject is voluminous and often contentious. A variety of different approaches and areas of emphasis are advocated, but such advocacy is based on relatively limited evidence. Advice for the counterinsurgent tends to be based on common sense, a general sense of history, or but one or two detailed historical cases. A broad base of evidentiary support for advocated approaches is lacking. This monograph and its companion, *Victory Has a Thousand Fathers: Detailed Counterinsurgency Case Studies*, seek to alleviate that

[1] Thomas X. Hammes, "Why Study Small Wars?" *Small Wars Journal*, Vol. 1, April 2005.

[2] William Rosenau, "Subversion and Terrorism: Understanding and Countering the Threat," in *The MIPT Terrorism Annual 2006*, Oklahoma City, Okla.: National Memorial Institute for the Prevention of Terrorism, 2006, p. 53.

deficit with thorough analyses based on a firm foundation of historical data. This is clearly an area that can benefit from extensive data collection, rigorous analysis, and empirical testing.

## Case Selection and Analytic Approach

This research quantitatively tested the performance of 20 distinct approaches to COIN against the recent historical record. Findings and analyses are based on detailed case studies compiled for 30 insurgencies. The locations, dates, and outcomes of these insurgencies appear in Figure S.1.

The selected cases are the 30 most recent resolved insurgencies.[3] In addition to being perfectly representative of the recent history of

**Figure S.1**
**Map of COIN Case Dates, Countries, and Outcomes**

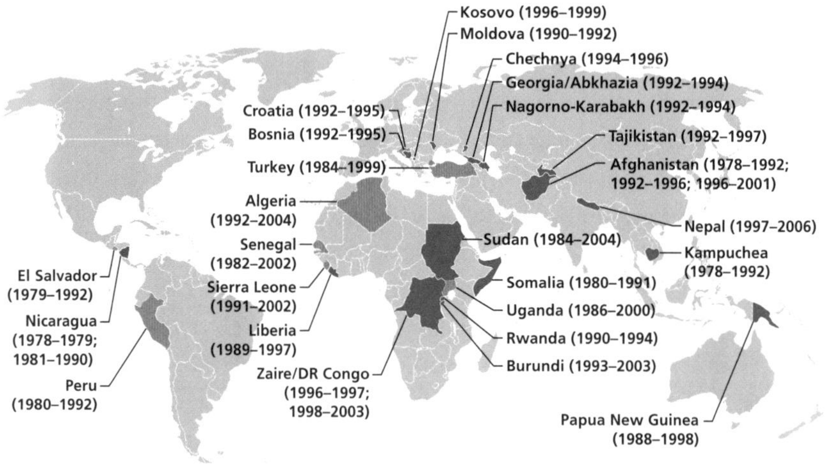


NOTE: Green shading indicates that the COIN force prevailed (or had the better of a mixed outcome), while red shading indicates that the outcome favored the insurgents (thus, a COIN loss).
RAND *MG964-S.1*

---

3 Only resolved cases were included because cases in which the outcome has yet to be determined are not useful for identifying the correlates of COIN success. After compiling a list of resolved insurgencies, we selected the 30 most recent by start date.

insurgency, these cases represent geographic variation (mountains, jungles, deserts, cities), regional and cultural variation (Africa, Latin America, Central Asia, the Balkans, the Far East), and variation in the military capabilities of COIN forces and insurgent forces alike.

Twenty distinct approaches to COIN, identified through a survey of the existing literature, were scrutinized through the lens of these 30 cases. Some of these approaches were drawn from classical perspectives on COIN from the previous century, such as pacification and cost-benefit; others are contemporary approaches suggested for ongoing operations in Iraq and Afghanistan, such as "boots on the ground" and the approach implicit in U.S. Army Field Manual (FM) 3-24, *Counterinsurgency*.[4] Also considered were practices advocated for the success of insurgents (as opposed to counterinsurgents).

## Key Findings

Because this research was vast in scope, the results are rich, detailed, and sometimes complicated. While different readers may find different aspects of our findings to be the most interesting or illuminating, this section presents six findings identified as key in formulating successful COIN operations.

### Effective COIN Practices Tend to Run in Packs

The first finding is the somewhat unsurprising observation that those who succeed in COIN operations do so by implementing a host of good COIN practices while avoiding adverse practices. This is wholly consonant with reports from commanders in both Iraq and Afghanistan that indicate success when engaging in numerous mutually reinforcing lines of operation. In the 30 cases studied here, the frequency

[4] Headquarters, U.S. Department of the Army, and Headquarters, U.S. Marine Corps, *Counterinsurgency Field Manual*, Field Manual 3-24/Marine Corps Warfighting Publication 3-33.5, Chicago, Ill.: University of Chicago Press, 2007. For simplicity, we refer to this publication as FM 3-24 or COIN FM throughout. For a review of classic approaches to COIN, see Austin Long, *On "Other War": Lessons from Five Decades of RAND Counterinsurgency Research*, Santa Monica, Calif.: RAND Corporation, MG-482-OSD, 2006.

with which good COIN practices occur in cases won by the government (COIN wins) and do not appear in cases won by the insurgents (COIN losses) is such that discrimination of any single practice as most important is impossible.

The "good" and "bad" COIN practices referred to were identified in one (or both) of two ways: first, based on a strong a priori grounding in existing COIN literature and research and, second, based on relationships observed in these data during preliminary analyses. Subsequent analyses validated these practices or factors as either positive or negative contributors to COIN outcomes (see Chapter Four for a full discussion). These factors are listed in Table S.1.

### The Balance of Good Versus Bad Practices Perfectly Predicts Outcomes

What *is* surprising is that the core finding that effective COIN practices run in packs holds across the 30 cases considered *without exception*. That is, every COIN win in the data (eight of 30 cases) has a strongly positive balance of successfully implemented good versus detrimental factors, and every COIN loss (22 of 30 cases) has a zero or negative balance of good versus detrimental factors. This is illustrated in Table S.2.

Table S.2 presents four pieces of information for each case: the sum of good COIN factors or practices during the decisive phase of the case (out of a maximum of 15), the sum of bad factors (out of a maximum of 12), the balance of the good factors minus the bad factors, and the outcome of the case.[5] The good and bad factors summed are the same as those listed in Table S.1. So, for instance, the very first row presents the post-Soviet insurgency in Afghanistan, in which the COIN force realized zero of 15 good factors and 10 of 12 bad factors, for a net balance of –10 and, unsurprisingly, a loss for the COIN force.

[5] Case outcome is from the perspective of the COIN force. "Loss" is a COIN loss, and "win" is a COIN win. Mixed outcomes have been attributed to the side most closely favored. For example, "mixed, favoring COIN" has been included in "win"; "mixed, favoring insurgents" has been included in "loss."

**Table S.1**
**"Good" and "Bad" COIN Practices or Factors**

| 15 Good COIN Practices | 12 Bad COIN Practices |
|---|---|
| The COIN force adhered to several strategic communication principles. | The COIN force used both collective punishment and escalating repression. |
| The COIN force significantly reduced tangible insurgent support. | The primary COIN force was an external occupier. |
| The government established or maintained legitimacy in the area of conflict. | COIN force or government actions contributed to substantial new grievances claimed by the insurgents. |
| The government was at least a partial democracy. | Militias worked at cross-purposes with the COIN force or government. |
| COIN force intelligence was adequate to support effective engagement or disruption of insurgents. | The COIN force resettled or removed civilian populations for population control. |
| The COIN force was of sufficient strength to force the insurgents to fight as guerrillas. | COIN force collateral damage was perceived by the population in the area of conflict as worse than the insurgents'. |
| The government/state was competent. | In the area of conflict, the COIN force was perceived as worse than the insurgents. |
| The COIN force avoided excessive collateral damage, disproportionate use of force, or other illegitimate applications of force. | The COIN force failed to adapt to changes in adversary strategy, operations, or tactics. |
| The COIN force sought to engage and establish positive relations with the population in the area of conflict. | The COIN force engaged in more coercion or intimidation than the insurgents. |
| Short-term investments, improvements in infrastructure or development, or property reform occurred in the area of conflict controlled or claimed by the COIN force. | The insurgent force was individually superior to the COIN force by being either more professional or better motivated. |
| The majority of the population in the area of conflict supported or favored the COIN force. | The COIN force or its allies relied on looting for sustainment. |
| The COIN force established and then expanded secure areas. | The COIN force and government had different goals or levels of commitment. |
| The COIN force had and used uncontested air dominance. | |
| The COIN force provided or ensured the provision of basic services in areas that it controlled or claimed to control. | |
| The perception of security was created or maintained among the population in areas that the COIN force claimed to control. | |

**Table S.2**
**Balance of Good COIN Practices and Bad COIN Practices for 30 Cases**

| Case | Good Factors (15) | Bad Factors (12) | Good – Bad Factors | Outcome |
|---|---|---|---|---|
| Afghanistan (post-Soviet) | 0 | 10 | –10 | Loss |
| Somalia | 1 | 10 | –9 | Loss |
| Chechnya I | 2 | 10 | –8 | Loss |
| Rwanda | 2 | 10 | –8 | Loss |
| Zaire (anti-Mobutu) | 0 | 8 | –8 | Loss |
| Nicaragua (Somoza) | 0 | 8 | –8 | Loss |
| Sudan (SPLA) | 2 | 9 | –7 | Loss |
| Kosovo | 1 | 8 | –7 | Loss |
| Afghanistan (anti-Soviet) | 1 | 7 | –6 | Loss |
| Papua New Guinea | 3 | 9 | –6 | Loss |
| Burundi | 2 | 8 | –6 | Loss |
| Bosnia | 1 | 6 | –5 | Loss |
| Moldova | 2 | 6 | –4 | Loss |
| Georgia/Abkhazia | 1 | 5 | –4 | Loss |
| Liberia | 3 | 7 | –4 | Loss |
| Afghanistan (Taliban) | 2 | 6 | –4 | Loss |
| Nagorno-Karabakh | 1 | 4 | –3 | Loss |
| DR Congo (anti-Kabila) | 1 | 4 | –3 | Loss |
| Tajikistan | 2 | 5 | –3 | Loss |
| Kampuchea | 1 | 3 | –2 | Loss |
| Nepal | 3 | 5 | –2 | Loss |
| Nicaragua (Contras) | 4 | 4 | 0 | Loss |
| Croatia | 8 | 3 | +5 | Win |
| Turkey (PKK) | 11 | 5 | +6 | Win |
| Uganda (ADF) | 8 | 0 | +8 | Win |
| Algeria (GIA) | 9 | 1 | +8 | Win |
| El Salvador | 12 | 2 | +10 | Win |
| Peru | 13 | 2 | +11 | Win |
| Senegal | 13 | 0 | +13 | Win |
| Sierra Leone | 14 | 1 | +13 | Win |

Table S.2 is sorted from low to high on net balance of good versus bad, which puts all the high scores (those with a positive balance of good versus bad) at the bottom of the table. All of the cases that have a positive balance of good versus bad factors were won by the COIN force; all those with a zero or negative balance were COIN force losses.

This key finding of the importance of a positive balance of good versus bad COIN practices is even more remarkable given that many of the conventional explanations of the outcomes of these cases rely on a narrative of exceptionality—that is, list one or more distinctive, exceptional, or "unique" aspects of the case's history that are critical to understanding the outcome.

These data show that, regardless of distinctiveness in the narrative and without exception, COIN forces that realize preponderantly more good than bad practices win, and those that do not lose. So, while every insurgency may be unique, that distinctiveness does not matter *at this level of analysis*. Successful implementation of identified good practices always allows the COIN force to prevail, independent of any uniqueness.[6]

### Of 20 COIN Approaches Tested, 13 Receive Strong Support, While Three Are Not Supported by Evidence

Unsurprisingly, much of the received wisdom on COIN is validated in this analysis. As part of the analysis, we reviewed the literature on COIN and identified 20 distinct approaches to these operations. We tested each approach against the empirical evidence provided by the 30 case studies. Of the 20 approaches tested, 13 receive strong empirical support, and a further two receive some support. Three approaches, however, are not supported by the evidence, and, in fact, the results provide strong evidence *against* them: resettlement, "crush them" (repression), and various insurgent support strategies. These results are summarized in Table S.3.

---

[6] This is not to say that contextual distinctions are not important. Successful implementation of an intended practice in the real world can be difficult indeed, and it can be highly contingent on the details of the situation.

Table S.3 lists each of the 20 approaches tested. From left to right, each row presents the summary name of the tested approach, the number of times the approach was implemented in a COIN loss (out of 22 cases that were COIN losses), the number of times the approach was implemented in a COIN win (out of eight COIN-winning cases),

**Table S.3**
**Strength of Evidentiary Support for 20 Approaches to COIN**

| Approach | COIN Losses Implementing Approach (of 22) | COIN Wins Implementing Approach (of 8) | Degree of Evidentiary Support |
|---|---|---|---|
| **Development** | **0** | **4** | **Strong support** |
| **Pacification** | **1** | **8** | **Strong support** |
| **Legitimacy (government)** | **3** | **7** | **Strong support** |
| Legitimacy (use of force) | 4 | 6 | Some support |
| Democracy | 7 | 8 | Some support |
| Resettlement | 8 | 1 | Strong evidence against |
| **Cost-benefit** | **2** | **8** | **Strong support** |
| **Border control** | **1** | **8** | **Strong support** |
| "Crush them" | 18 | 2 | Strong evidence against |
| Amnesty/rewards | 0 | 5 | Cannot be tested |
| **Strategic communication** | **2** | **8** | **Strong support** |
| **COIN FM** | **1** | **7** | **Strong support** |
| **"Beat cop"** | **4** | **8** | **Strong support** |
| **"Boots on the ground"** | **2** | **6** | **Strong support** |
| "Put a local face on it" | NA | NA | Cannot be tested |
| Cultural awareness | NA | NA | Cannot be tested |
| **Tangible support reduction** | **0** | **8** | **Strong support** |
| **Criticality of intelligence** | **0** | **6** | **Strong support** |
| **Flexibility and adaptability** | **6** | **8** | **Strong support** |
| Insurgent support strategies | 22 | 7 | Strong evidence against |
| **Continuation and contestation** | **18** | **0** | **Strong support** |

and the degree of support provided by the evidence. We considered approaches to COIN strongly supported if the relationship between the presence of the approach and the case outcome was very strong (using it and it alone is a very strong indicator of the outcome); "some support" indicates that the relationship is strong but the approach's application results in a significant number of losses; and "strong evidence against" means that the approach's application predicts a greater proportion of losses than wins. An approach was considered untestable if it was never applied.[7]

Next, we provide detailed results for two of these approaches, which merit special attention.

### Repression Wins Phases, but Usually Not Cases

While some repressive COIN forces have managed to prevail, this analysis shows unambiguously that repression is a bad COIN practice. Only two of eight COIN winners used escalating repression and collective punishment during the decisive phase of the conflict: Turkey and Croatia. While these two COIN forces employed repression, they also employed a pack of good COIN practices, apparently enough to offset the negative impact of repression.

Repression was shown to win intermediate phases, but in these case studies, the vast majority of phases won with repression preceded ultimate defeat in the case. This occurs over and over in the data. Fourteen of 22 cases in which the insurgents prevailed include an intermediate phase in which the COIN force used escalating repression and collective punishment to temporarily take the upper hand on its way to defeat. Examples include all three Afghanistan cases, Somalia, Burundi, Tajikistan, and Kosovo. While it is possible to find examples

[7] Two of the approaches, "put a local face on it" and cultural awareness, are corollaries to broader approaches that are only applicable when the primary COIN force is an external force. The primary COIN force was composed of outsiders in only three of the 30 cases informing this analysis, and the factors for "put a local face on it" and cultural awareness were present in none of these three cases. There is thus insufficient evidence to test these two approaches in any way. Similarly, the way in which the amnesty/reward approach was operationalized created possible causal conflation and precluded definitive results.

of success in COIN through repression, they are either exceptions or short-term victories.

### Tangible Support Trumps Popular Support

The ability of the insurgents to replenish and obtain personnel, materiel, financing, intelligence, and sanctuary (tangible support) perfectly predicts success or failure in the 30 COIN cases considered here. In all eight cases in which the COIN force prevailed, it also disrupted at least three tangible insurgent support factors, while none of the COIN forces in the 22 losing cases managed to disrupt more than two.

**How does tangible support relate to popular support?** In 25 of the 30 cases, popular support and tangible support ran parallel. That is, if the majority of the population in the area of conflict wanted the COIN force to win (our operationalization of popular support), the COIN force was able to disrupt at least three tangible support factors; if the insurgents had majority popular support, the COIN force was unable to significantly reduce tangible support. This finding is consonant with population-centric approaches to COIN. When needed tangible support comes primarily from the population, popular support is the center of gravity.

**What happens when popular support and tangible support diverge?** In five of the 30 historical insurgencies, tangible support did not follow popular support. In three cases (Moldova, Rwanda, and Tajikistan), the COIN force had the support of the majority of the population but failed to significantly reduce the insurgents' tangible support (which was primarily coming from supporters outside the three countries). In all three of these cases, the COIN force lost. In two cases (Turkey and Croatia), the COIN force did not have the support of the majority of the population in the area of conflict but managed to significantly reduce tangible support to the insurgents anyway. In both of those cases, the COIN force prevailed.

This suggests an important caveat to population-centric COIN approaches: The population is the center of gravity if the population is the primary source of insurgents' tangible support. When insurgents' tangible support needs are being met elsewhere, a successful campaign will require additional areas of emphasis.

### Poor Beginnings Do Not Necessarily Lead to Poor Ends

These analyses show that getting off to a poor start in the early phases of a conflict does not necessarily lead to a COIN loss. Of the eight cases won by the COIN force, in only two cases were the outcomes of all phases favorable to the COIN force (Senegal and Croatia). In fact, in three of the cases won by the COIN force, the COIN force had the upper hand only in the decisive phase (Peru, Sierra Leone, and Uganda). Changing practices can lead to changed outcomes.

## Recommendations

Taken together, these findings suggest two primary recommendations for those preparing to undertake COIN:

1. *Plan to pursue multiple mutually supporting lines of operation in COIN.*
2. *Build and maintain forces that are capable of engaging in multiple mutually supporting lines of operation simultaneously.*

COIN forces that prevail over insurgencies *all* register a considerable positive balance of positive practices and activities over detracting practices. Not every positive approach attempted by the COIN force will actually be successfully realized in practice. There is no hard-and-fast threshold for the minimum number of good COIN practices in which a COIN force must engage to win. The various good COIN practices identified here are not conducted in sequence; they are conducted simultaneously. If one is serious about supporting or conducting COIN, one must be prepared to engage in as many of the identified good COIN practices as possible, for as long as necessary.

For the broader U.S. government, this means that U.S. COIN efforts must be sufficiently resourced, in terms of both staffing and other support, to give multiple areas of endeavor the attention needed. Further, non–U.S. Department of Defense (DoD) partner agencies must be sufficiently robust to contribute to development, governance, and legitimacy, and their activities must be coordinated with DoD

COIN operations. For DoD, this means rejecting out of hand any proposal or plan that emphasizes a single COIN approach or other "magic bullet" at the expense of other positive practices. Current best practices with regard to mutually supporting lines of operation from Iraq and Afghanistan must be carried forward into future contingency planning. While commanders who have served in contemporary operations intuitively accept the importance of multiple mutually supporting lines of operation to successful COIN, this intuition must be incorporated into the institutional memory of U.S. defense organizations—in joint and service doctrine both for planning and in areas that are specific to COIN or irregular warfare. Finally, these first two recommendations will require DoD to establish and maintain increased capabilities in the areas of building partner capacity, civil affairs and reconstruction, and information and influence operations.

3. *Ensure the positive involvement of the host-nation government.*

Several of the empirically supported approaches (e.g., democracy, government legitimacy, strategic communication) and several of the items on the list of good COIN practices depend on the nature and behavior of the host-nation government. If a host-nation government or its structure and practices do not comport with good COIN practices, all possible pressure should be brought to bear to ensure government reform. Failure to realize the good COIN practices associated with government, governance, and legitimacy leaves available significantly fewer members of the pack of good COIN practices and leaves no guarantee that victory remains possible. The United States should think twice before choosing to help governments that will not help themselves.

4. *Keep a scorecard of good versus bad factors and practices; if the balance does not correspond to the desired outcome, make changes.*

Table S.2 shows that, without exception, winning COIN forces had a significant positive balance of good practices relative to bad practices, and losing COIN forces had a zero or negative balance. When engaging in COIN operations, as dispassionately and accurately as possible, assess the presence or absence of the factors listed in Table S.1, and add them up. Is the COIN force where it should be (remembering that the lowest-scoring COIN winner had a balance of five)? If not, change strategies (or implementation approaches). A blank scorecard can be found at the end of this volume.

5. *Recognize that there is time to adapt.*

Obviously, it would be better to start with and stick with good COIN practices, but that is sometimes easier said than done, especially when working by, with, or through partner nations. Just because a COIN or COIN-support operation gets off to a seemingly poor start, do not abandon the intention of following good COIN practices. Of the eight winning COIN forces in our case studies, only two (Senegal and Croatia) won every phase of the conflict. Three of the winners (Peru, Sierra Leone, and Uganda) won only the final phase. Getting off to a bad start does not doom a COIN operation. Recognize that providing support for a struggling COIN operation or reinvesting in a failing one is not a strategically quixotic or doomed endeavor.

Our fifth recommendation has important implications for balancing risk. If future scenarios include the possibility of major combat operations against a peer or near-peer adversary, failure to adequately program for that contingency is an unacceptable risk. Loss in such a conflict could be unbearably costly for the nation. If futures include COIN operations (and any plausible future must), the risk associated with being insufficiently prepared for such operations is lower: Operations may face initial setbacks and may take longer to see ultimate resolution, but initial failure does not necessitate ultimate failure—there is time to adapt. Risk calculation–based allocations must be mindful not only of the relatively greater likelihood of COIN operations than major combat operations against near-peer adversaries but also of the relatively lower levels of risk associated with initial shortcomings in the former.

6. *Avoid using and discourage allies and partners from using repression and collective punishment in COIN.*

Our analyses strongly suggest that repression is a poor COIN practice. Only two of eight COIN winners used repressive practices in the decisive phase of their cases, and they offset the negative impact by employing a host of good practices. Consider the case of Tajikistan in the mid-1990s, in which the Tajik government and its Russian allies aggressively and indiscriminately beat back an initially successful insurgency, temporarily gaining the upper hand but further alienating the population by ignoring its needs, grievances, and well-being. Repression can win phases by dealing the insurgents a blow and making support for the insurgents more costly for supporters, but our data show that the vast majority of phases that were won with repression ultimately increased popular support for the insurgency and ended in a COIN defeat for the entire case.

U.S. military doctrine and practice preclude the use of disproportionate force or collective punishment, so this is not a concern with regard to U.S. forces. However, all possible partners and allies do not share this prohibition. When joining allies or establishing or reestablishing partner security forces (or militias), all possible care should be taken to ensure that they maintain proper respect for human rights and have a full understanding of the likely long-term consequences of routine disproportionate or illegitimate uses of force. If partners are unlikely to adhere to these standards, they should be avoided as partners.

7. *Ascertain the specific support needs of and sources of support for insurgent adversaries and target them.*

When insurgents draw their support primarily from the population, a primarily population-focused set of COIN strategies should work. When insurgents' support comes from external actors (or other sources), then approaches explicitly targeting that supply chain are necessary, along with efforts to win over the population. DoD should ensure that this strategic and operational imperative is prominent in future plans and doctrine.

## Acknowledgments

Andrew Caldwell, our principal point of contact in OSD(CAPE)IW, and Matthew Minatelli in the Office of the Under Secretary of Defense for Policy provided critical support to, encouragement of, and confidence in this research effort as it grew from something quite modest into something much more substantial over the project's two years. We thank them both for their active participation in formulating and sustaining this research. We owe Timothy Bright, director of OSD(CAPE)IW, a debt of gratitude for his willingness to support foundational research with little direct and immediate application to the day-to-day challenges his office faces. We hope the host of interesting findings herein rewards that choice.

Our thanks go to RAND colleague Martin Libicki for the list of insurgencies from which we selected our case studies. Thanks, too, to Jefferson Marquis for his intellectual contributions in early conversations and his comments on a late draft. Quality assurance reviewers Daniel Byman, John Gordon, and Charles Ragin all provided feedback that strengthened the final product. We also wish to acknowledge the contributions of RAND administrative assistant Maria Falvo and communication analyst Kate Giglio, without whom the presentation of this monograph would be less accessible and the citations less complete. Finally, we thank editor Lauren Skrabala, production editor Jocelyn Lofstrom, and artists Maritta Tapanainen and Mary Wrazen for their work in producing the final document.

Omissions and errors remain the responsibility of the authors alone.

# Abbreviations

| | |
|---|---|
| ADF | Allied Democratic Forces |
| CIA | Central Intelligence Agency |
| COIN | counterinsurgency |
| DoD | U.S. Department of Defense |
| DRC | Democratic Republic of the Congo |
| ECOMOG | Economic Community of West African States Monitoring Group |
| ECOWAS | Economic Community of West African States |
| EO | Executive Outcomes |
| FDD | Forces for the Defense of Democracy |
| FM | field manual |
| FMLN | Frente Farabundo Martí para la Liberación Nacional [Farabundo Martí National Liberation Front] |
| fsQCA | fuzzy-set Qualitative Comparative Analysis (software) |
| GIA | Groupe Islamique Armé [Armed Islamic Group] |
| HV | Hrvatska Vojska [Croatian army] |

| | |
|---|---|
| IO | information operations |
| JNA | Jugoslavenska Narodna Armija [Yugoslav People's Army] |
| KLA | Kosovo Liberation Army |
| MFDC | Mouvement des Forces Démocratiques de la Casamance [Movement of Democratic Forces of the Casamance] |
| NATO | North Atlantic Treaty Organization |
| NPFL | National Patriotic Front of Liberia |
| OSD(CAPE)IW | Office of the Secretary of Defense, Cost Analysis and Program Evaluation, Irregular Warfare Division |
| PKK | Parti Karkerani Kurdistan [Kurdistan Workers' Party] |
| PSYOP | psychological operations |
| QCA | qualitative comparative analysis |
| RPF | Rwandan Patriotic Front |
| SNM | Somali National Movement |
| SPLA | Sudan People's Liberation Army |
| SSDF | Somali Salvation Democratic Front |
| UN | United Nations |
| UNAMSIL | United Nations Mission in Sierra Leone |
| UTO | United Tajik Opposition |

CHAPTER ONE

# Introduction

> "Victory has a thousand fathers, but defeat is an orphan."
>
> —*John Fitzgerald Kennedy*

## Purpose of This Study

As the United States, China, Israel, India, Russia, and other countries seek to modernize their military forces and upgrade already potent weapon systems, the gap between conventional and unconventional forces will continue to widen. As a result of this growing disparity, insurgents, terrorists, and militias are likely to become an increasingly common foe.[1] Insurgency is a timeless mode of conflict and has taken many forms: independence movements during decolonization, ethnic/sectarian conflict, regional separatism, and resistance to occupation. We need look no further than contemporary operations to see the United States and its allies opposing insurgencies in both Iraq and Afghanistan. *When a country becomes host to an insurgency, which counterinsurgency (COIN) approaches give the government the best chance of prevailing?* This question is the principal inquiry addressed in this monograph and in the accompanying volume of case studies.[2]

---

[1] Michael T. Klare notes that, of the 50 armed conflicts that broke out in the 1990s, only four entailed combat between two or more states, and only one, the Persian Gulf War, involved all-out fighting among large numbers of air, ground, and sea forces (Michael T. Klare, "The New Face of Combat: Terrorism and Irregular Warfare in the 21st Century," in Charles W. Kegley, Jr., ed., *The New Global Terrorism: Characteristics, Causes, Controls*, Upper Saddle River, N.J.: Prentice Hall, 2003, p. 29).

[2] See Paul, Clarke, and Grill, 2010.

Contemporary discourse is rife with recommended approaches to COIN and advice for would-be counterinsurgents. Scholars, observers, and theorists—amateur and professional alike—draw on history, common sense, or contemporary operations to recommend certain COIN practices and disparage others. Communities of interested military and nonmilitary personnel engage in vigorous debates about the effectiveness of various approaches to COIN or the applicability of a certain proponent's proposals in specific contexts.[3] Much of the discussion and theorizing is founded on individuals' personal experiences with insurgency, their detailed analysis of one or two historical cases, or their general sense of history. While existing approaches and discussions clearly contain good advice for COIN forces, there remain substantial disagreement and dispute. How are we to adjudicate between partially conflicting approaches and contradictory advice? We want to learn the lessons of history, but of which lessons and which histories should we be most mindful?

One of our chief findings is that those who succeed in COIN do so by implementing a host of good COIN practices while avoiding those that are adverse. While we were unable to discern any single most important COIN practice, the data suggest that good practices occur together (along with success) with such regularity that we cannot even rank their importance. Victory, it appears, does indeed have a thousand fathers—a substantial collection of effective practices and a host of complementary and mutually reinforcing lines of operation is what wins the day in COIN. These practices are the subject of this volume and the lens through which we examine 30 case studies of recent COIN operations.[4]

---

[3] See, for example, the wide range of articles, opinions, and (most of all) discussions that have taken place on the *Small Wars Journal* blog.

[4] Detailed narratives and data for the 30 case studies are presented in Paul, Clarke, and Grill, 2010.

## Data and Analyses

The research presented here tests against the record of history 20 distinct approaches to or pieces of practical advice for COIN drawn from the existing COIN literature. Moving beyond validation through one or two case studies, this research assembles a significant and systematic empirical foundation from which to assess COIN approaches: detailed case studies of the 30 most recent resolved insurgencies worldwide.[5] These cases and their selection are described in Chapter Two. Our findings provide strong empirical support for some approaches to COIN and strong evidence against others, as discussed in Chapter Three.

By analyzing the patterns of practices and factors that are characteristic of COIN wins and COIN losses in these 30 cases, we move beyond the testing of recommended approaches to COIN. We develop a list of "good" and "bad" factors based, first, on strong a priori grounding in existing COIN literature and, second, on relationships observed in our data during preliminary analyses. Based on the patterns of presence or absence of these practices and factors in the 30 cases, we reach several interesting conclusions, including the aforementioned "good COIN practices tend to run in packs." Details of these analyses are presented in Chapter Four.

## About This Monograph and the Accompanying Case Studies

The balance of this monograph is organized as follows. Chapter Two describes the methods used to identify the 30 most recently begun, concluded cases of insurgency; details how we collected data for these cases; and presents brief historical summaries of the 30 cases. Chapter Three introduces the 20 distinct approaches to COIN iden-

---

[5] This broad empirical basis allows us to avoid three logical traps that much of the contemporary debate fails to escape: (1) the trap of ongoing operations (what we are seeing now is what we will always see); (2) the trap of individual cases (what happened in one particular case tells us about what could or should happen in all cases); and (3) the trap of bad analogy (every U.S. COIN effort is like Vietnam).

tified from the literature, describes the factors that represent them in the analysis, and tests them against the record of history by considering the impact of implementation of those approaches on the outcomes of the 30 cases. Chapter Four provides analyses of the impact on case outcomes due to different *patterns* of practices and factors that are present or absent in the cases. That chapter also discusses the development and validation of a list of "good" and "bad" COIN practices and our attempt to mathematically reduce the host of strongly supported approaches to COIN to a minimally sufficient set. Chapter Five draws conclusions and makes recommendations.

The report is supported by three appendixes and an accompanying volume of case studies. Appendix A provides extensive methodological details supporting our analyses. Appendix B provides the technical details of one of the analyses conducted as part of the research, qualitative comparative analysis. Appendix C offers and discusses possible criticisms of the analysis and the approach. A separate volume, *Victory Has a Thousand Fathers: Detailed Counterinsurgency Case Studies*, contains a case narrative for each of the 30 COIN cases, along with a tabular presentation of the data scores for all factors for each phase of each case.[6]

---

6 See Paul, Clarke, and Grill, 2010.

CHAPTER TWO

# The Cases

Thirty cases of insurgency form the empirical foundation for this research. This chapter begins by describing the process used to select the cases and to collect data for them, as well as how we determined whether the outcome of a case was a win or a loss for COIN forces. The bulk of the chapter, however, is devoted to brief summaries of each of the 30 cases. More extensive case-study details can be found in the accompanying volume, *Victory Has a Thousand Fathers: Detailed Counterinsurgency Case Studies.*[1]

## Case Selection and Data Collection

The 30 insurgency cases were drawn from a larger list of historical insurgencies developed as part of a previous RAND COIN study.[2] That initial list included 89 cases and purports to be an exhaustive list of insurgencies from 1934 to 2008. All cases met the following criteria:

---

1 Paul, Clarke, and Grill, 2010.

2 Martin C. Libicki, "Eighty-Nine Insurgencies: Outcomes and Endings," in David C. Gompert, John Gordon IV, Adam Grissom, David R. Frelinger, Seth G. Jones, Martin C. Libicki, Edward O'Connell, Brooke Stearns Lawson, and Robert E. Hunter, *War by Other Means—Building Complete and Balanced Capabilities for Counterinsurgency: RAND Counterinsurgency Study—Final Report*, Santa Monica, Calif.: RAND Corporation, MG-595/2-OSD, 2008. The initial case list was drawn from James D. Fearon and David D. Laitin, "Ethnicity, Insurgency, and Civil War," *American Political Science Review*, Vol. 97, No. 1, February 2003.

- They involved fighting between states and nonstates seeking to take control of a government or region or that used violence to change government policies.
- The conflict killed at least 1,000 people over its course, with a yearly average of at least 100.
- At least 100 people were killed on both sides (including civilians attacked by rebels).
- They were not coups, countercoups, or insurrections.

From that list, we selected the 30 most recently begun, completed cases for our study. Selection of these 30 cases also corresponds to a 30-year chronological span: All insurgencies began and were resolved between 1978 and 2008. These 30 cases span 26 countries and much of the globe (see Figure 2.1). Appendix A includes further detail about the case selection.

**Figure 2.1**
**Map of COIN Case Dates, Countries, and Outcomes**

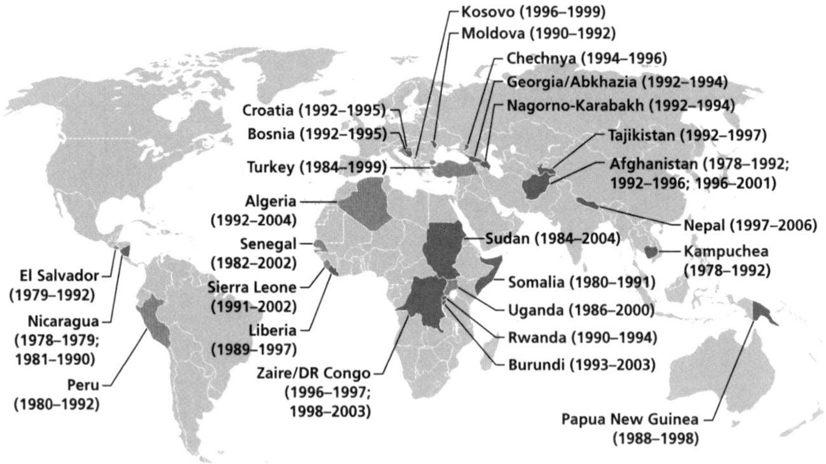


NOTE: Green shading indicates that the COIN force prevailed (or had the better of a mixed outcome), while red shading indicates that the outcome favored the insurgents (thus, a COIN loss).
RAND *MG964-2.1*

Data for the case studies come from secondary sources. The analyst assigned to each case thoroughly reviewed the available English-language history and secondary analysis of the conflict for that case. Documentation proved voluminous for some cases (particularly those in Central and South America but also cases in which Russian or Soviet forces were involved); it was much more sparse for other cases (particularly those in Africa). In all cases, available information was sufficient to meet our data needs for the quantitative analyses (described in Chapters Three and Four). The references provided at the end of the accompanying volume of case studies demonstrate the range and depth of the available literature.

## Phased Data

Because the approach and behavior of the COIN force, the actions of insurgents, and other important conditions can all change during the course of an insurgency, we broke all of the cases into two to five phases. Throughout the discussion, *case data* refers to the data for the decisive phase of the case. A detailed discussion of each phase of each case and the value of each quantitative factor can be found in the accompanying volume, *Victory Has a Thousand Fathers: Detailed Counterinsurgency Case Studies.*[3] Appendix A includes additional discussion of the phase assignment process in the section "Phased Data."

The phases are not of uniform duration. A new phase was declared when the case analyst recognized a significant shift in the COIN approach, in the approach of the insurgents, or in the exogenous conditions of the case. Phases were *not* intended to capture micro-changes or tiny cycles of adaptation and counteradaptation between the insurgents and the COIN force; rather, these were macro-level and sea-change phases.

---

[3] Paul, Clarke, and Grill, 2010.

## Assessing Case Outcomes

Since our analysis focuses on correlates of success in COIN, one of the most important elements of our case studies is the identification of the outcome of the cases (i.e., whether COIN forces actually succeeded). Many of these cases have complicated outcomes in which neither side realized all of its stated objectives and it is not exactly clear who won. While we report mixed outcomes in our case narratives, we also identify each case as either a COIN win or a COIN loss.

To adjudicate unclear case outcomes, we followed the logic illustrated in Figure 2.2. First, for each case, we asked whether the government against which the insurgency arose had stayed in power through the end of the conflict and whether it retained sovereignty over the region of conflict. If insurgents either deposed (or otherwise led to the fall of) the government or won de facto control of a separatist region, then the COIN force did *not* win. If the government remained in power and the country remained intact, then we further considered whether the government had been forced to (or chose to) make major concessions to the insurgents, such as power sharing or loss of territory or other sovereign control, or was otherwise forced to yield to insurgent demands. If the government stayed in power, the country remained intact, and no major concessions were granted to the insurgents, then the COIN force unambiguously won. If, however, major concessions were made, then the outcome was mixed. In all cases, what constituted a "major" concession and who (the COIN force or the insurgents) had the better of a mixed outcome was decided at the discretion of the individual case analyst and was based on the distinct narrative of that case.

Applying this logic to the 30 selected cases results in eight cases that are COIN wins and 22 cases that are COIN losses. Table 2.1 lists the insurgencies, the dates they spanned, and their outcomes.

The remainder of this chapter presents brief summaries of the historical cases. They are presented by start date. Analyses of the relationships between specific approaches and factors and case outcomes are presented in Chapters Three and Four. Those familiar with the histories of these cases are welcome to skip ahead.

**Figure 2.2**
**Logic for Assignment of Case Outcomes**

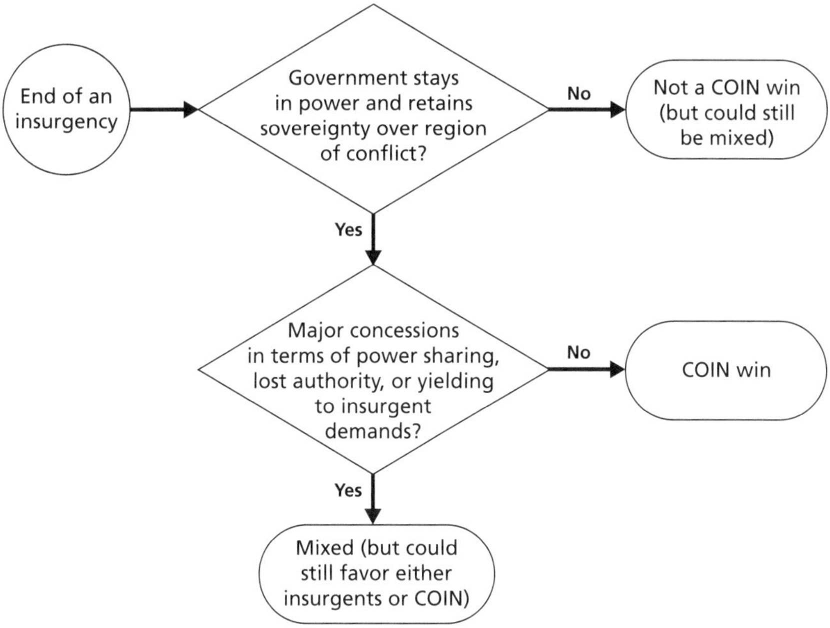


RAND *MG964-2.2*

**Table 2.1**
**Countries, Insurgents, and Date Spans of the 30 Case-Study Insurgencies**

| Country (Insurgency) | Years | Outcome |
|---|---|---|
| Nicaragua (Somoza) | 1978–1979 | COIN loss |
| Afghanistan (anti-Soviet) | 1978–1992 | COIN loss |
| Kampuchea | 1978–1992 | COIN loss |
| El Salvador | 1979–1992 | **COIN win** |
| Somalia | 1980–1991 | COIN loss |
| Peru | 1980–1992 | **COIN win** |
| Nicaragua (Contras) | 1981–1990 | COIN loss |
| Senegal | 1982–2002 | **COIN win** |
| Turkey (PKK) | 1984–1999 | **COIN win** |
| Sudan (SPLA) | 1984–2004 | COIN loss |

**Table 2.1—Continued**

| Country (Insurgency) | Years | Outcome |
|---|---|---|
| Uganda (ADF) | 1986–2000 | **COIN win** |
| Papua New Guinea | 1988–1998 | COIN loss |
| Liberia | 1989–1997 | COIN loss |
| Rwanda | 1990–1994 | COIN loss |
| Moldova | 1990–1992 | COIN loss |
| Sierra Leone | 1991–2002 | **COIN win** |
| Algeria (GIA) | 1992–2004 | **COIN win** |
| Croatia | 1992–1995 | **COIN win** |
| Afghanistan (post-Soviet) | 1992–1996 | COIN loss |
| Tajikistan | 1992–1997 | COIN loss |
| Georgia/Abkhazia | 1992–1994 | COIN loss |
| Nagorno-Karabakh | 1992–1994 | COIN loss |
| Bosnia | 1992–1995 | COIN loss |
| Burundi | 1993–2003 | COIN loss |
| Chechnya I | 1994–1996 | COIN loss |
| Afghanistan (Taliban) | 1996–2001 | COIN loss |
| Zaire (anti-Mobutu) | 1996–1997 | COIN loss |
| Kosovo | 1996–1999 | COIN loss |
| Nepal | 1997–2006 | COIN loss |
| DR Congo (anti-Kabila) | 1998–2003 | COIN loss |

NOTE: "COIN loss" includes the outcomes "insurgent win" and "mixed, favoring insurgents" (nine of 22 case losses were mixed outcomes favoring the insurgents). "COIN win" includes "COIN win" and "mixed, favoring COIN force." "Mixed, favoring COIN force" occurs only once in the eight COIN wins. For details on outcome scoring and categories, see the section "Outcome Assessment" in Appendix A.

## Nicaragua (Somoza), 1978–1979

*Case Outcome: COIN Loss*

Four decades of neopatrimonial rule by a corrupt and unpopular government led to an uprising in the rural parts of Nicaragua that quickly spread from the countryside to the cities and towns surrounding the capital, Managua. The murder of Pedro Joaquín Chamorro, an extremely popular newspaper editor, served to add fuel to an already smoldering fire as widespread dissatisfaction with the Somoza regime quickly galvanized into an insurgency.

Four important factors converged to allow the insurgents to dislodge a qualitatively and quantitatively superior COIN force. First, the three main insurgent groups reconciled their respective differences and combined their efforts to fight the government. Second, indiscriminate violence by the counterinsurgents turned the population toward the Sandinistas and swelled their ranks with recruits. Third, the Carter administration decided that it could no longer back Nicaraguan president Anastasio Somoza Debayle following egregious human rights violations committed by his forces. Finally, Venezuela, Cuba, and Panama afforded the insurgency the weapons and safe haven necessary to defeat a stronger opponent. The combination of effective political organization by the Sandinistas, repressive policies by the government, loss of support for Somoza in the United States, and a steady supply of weapons from various Latin American nations to the insurgents led to an insurgent victory in a short but bloody conflict.

**Afghanistan (Anti-Soviet), 1978–1992**

*Outcome: COIN Loss*

The Afghan insurgency against the Soviet Union has been referred to as a "textbook study of how a major power can fail to win a war against guerrillas."[4] Despite their overwhelming political and military superiority, the Soviets encountered unexpected opposition to their invasion in 1979 and were unprepared to face the challenge of sustaining a weak, unpopular communist government against highly motivated Islamic fighters, or mujahadeen. While Moscow and its proxy regime in Kabul were able to develop more effective COIN policies in the mid-1980s, they were at a disadvantage against the mujahadeen, who not only benefited from extensive external support (including the provision of highly effective Stinger missiles from the United States) and reli-

[4] Anthony James Joes, *Guerrilla Warfare: A Historical, Biographical, and Bibliographical Sourcebook*, Westport, Conn.: Greenwood Press, 1996, p. 119.

gious fervor but were also in a position to "win by simply not losing."[5] The mujahadeen failed to unify as an insurgent force or offer an alternative form of governance, yet they were able to delegitimize the Kabul regime and defeat the Soviets after more than a decade of guerrilla war.

### Kampuchea, 1978–1992

*Case Outcome: COIN Loss (Mixed, Favoring Insurgents)*

Fed up with the policies and cross-border incursions of Kampuchea's Khmer Rouge government, Vietnam invaded Kampuchea in December 1978. Initially welcomed for freeing the people of Cambodia from the depredations of Pol Pot, the Vietnamese quickly wore out their welcome. With the support of Thailand (and others further abroad), the Khmer Rouge reconstituted itself as a significant insurgency, and several other insurgent movements formed and contested the occupation. The 1984–1985 dry season saw the Vietnamese and their Cambodian proxies aggressively sweep the border regions free of insurgents and then build a "bamboo curtain" (with cleared ground, minefields, and defensive road networks) with their K5 plan. This ambitious operation was effective over the short term, but the bamboo curtain did not keep the insurgents out, and the use of forced labor in its construction further alienated the population. After several years of expensive stalemate, Vietnamese forces abandoned Cambodia to their indigenous proxies in 1989. The puppet government managed to hang on through the signing of the Paris Peace Agreement in 1991 and into the United Nations (UN) peacekeeping mission period. It was then soundly defeated at the polls.

Although the government unambiguously lost this insurgency, it is scored as a mixed outcome for two reasons. First, the principal insurgent group, the Khmer Rouge, also "lost" in that it was not particularly favored in the settlement or an important part of the postconflict governing coalition (other, more modestly sized and more moderate insurgent groups were). Second, although it withdrew and its puppet

[5] The phrase "win by not losing," which has been used to characterize the goals of the Afghan resistance, is a central tenet of the "continuation and contestation" approach (see Chapter Four).

government was ultimately displaced, the government of Vietnam realized many of its more modest long-term political goals for Cambodia.

### El Salvador, 1979–1992

*Case Outcome: COIN Win (Mixed, Favoring COIN)*

The Farabundo Martí National Liberation Front (FMLN) offered a significant challenge to a kleptocratic and dictatorial Salvadoran government and a corrupt, barracks-bound Salvadoran military whose only significant victories were against the civilian population. With time bought by massive amounts of U.S. aid during the 1980s, the government of El Salvador democratized and increased its legitimacy, while the military increased its competence and improved its respect for human rights. By the end of the conflict, real evidence of reform corresponded with government and military statements and helped generate and sustain credibility and legitimacy. The conflict reached a stalemate in the late 1980s and was ultimately resolved through a settlement favorable to the government as external support to the insurgents dwindled and participation in the political process became an increasingly tenable approach to redressing grievances.

### Somalia, 1980–1991

*Case Outcome: COIN Loss*

Mohamed Siad Barre's dictatorial regime was ousted by a decade-long insurgency that featured several insurgent groups fighting against the government. COIN forces repeatedly resorted to brutal tactics, which only served to galvanize the opposition and turn local populations against the military. Barre continuously underestimated the threat posed by the various insurgent factions while also failing to take heed of growing antigovernment sentiment among average Somalis. After years of wanton violence against civilians and any persons thought to be associated with certain tribes, Barre's government lost any support it once had, and the population actively supported the various insurgent groups in their quest to overthrow the dictator.

As the insurgency progressed, the two main insurgent groups operating in the north, the Somali National Movement (SNM) and the Somali Salvation Democratic Front (SSDF), began to capture territory throughout the country. Moreover, the SNM received material support from neighboring Ethiopia. Growing discord between Barre's regime and the military, coupled with a lack of a coherent COIN approach, contributed to his downfall. No longer able to bribe and coerce the myriad clans and tribes he had tactfully manipulated for so long, and facing a more organized and aggressive insurgency, Barre eventually succumbed to defeat as he fled the country in the wake of his government's collapse. Somalia's clan- and tribal-based society was an ideal setting for guerrilla warfare, and the country has not had a functioning government since 1991.

### Peru, 1980–1992

*Case Outcome: COIN Win*

Abimael Guzmán's Sendero Luminoso, or Shining Path, proved to be a surprisingly resilient threat to democratic Peru. Arising in the midst of a significant economic crisis that corrupt and squabbling government officials did little to resolve, Sendero was first treated as a law-enforcement problem. The threat grew largely unabated until 1982, when states of emergency were declared in many of the country's departments, allowing the military to enter the conflict. Massive repression and indiscriminant violence did little to help the government's cause. The late 1980s saw shifts in government strategies, with reduced repression and new attempts to encourage development. These initiatives were marred, however, by corruption and lack of unity of effort. Though Sendero never had the support of most of the population (the group was too violent and too radical), government and military incompetence led to widespread belief that the insurgents would win. All this changed with the 1990 election of Alberto Fujimori to the presidency and his administration's commitment to local defense forces and an intelligence-focused strategy that ultimately led to the capture of Guzmán and the disintegration of Sendero. Under Fujimori, for the first time in the conflict, the government, police, and military made effective use of what would now be called *strategic communication*, with a greater emphasis on government credibility and consistency between actions and messages.

**Nicaragua (Contras), 1981–1990**

*Case Outcome: COIN Loss*

Various opposition groups came together to fight against the Sandinista government shortly after its victory over the Somoza regime in late 1979. This insurgency is heralded as classic example of the Reagan Doctrine in action. Backed by the Central Intelligence Agency (CIA), Contra insurgents gained momentum early in the conflict by catching the Sandinistas by surprise. After regrouping and improving intelligence collection during the second phase of the insurgency, the Sandinistas regained the upper hand. Ultimately, however, the Contras emerged victorious as a result of better training and organization, as well as considerable pressure exerted on the Sandinista government by the United States. Militarily, the support provided by the United States in the form of training, weapons, and money allowed the Contras to avoid defeat just long enough for the political elements of the insurgency to work in their favor. Politically, the U.S.-backed candidate, Violeta Chamorro, benefitted significantly from the nearly $3 million spent by the National Endowment for Democracy on "technical assistance."

**Senegal, 1982–2002**

*Case Outcome: COIN Win*

A separatist insurgency, the Movement of Democratic Forces of the Casamance (MFDC), troubled the government of Senegal for two full decades. Early on, the group "capitalized upon the grievances of the local populations, and received support from them."[6] However, in the early 1990s, the insurgency began receiving external support from neighboring countries the Gambia and Guinea-Bissau, which led it to escalate its tactics and turn on the local population. As the government of Senegal sought to improve relations with its neighbors in an effort to stem the flow of support for the insurgency, it also attempted to cut off any remaining internal support for the MFDC through what Wagane Faye has called a "politics of 'charm.'" (Senegal is the only case in which

[6] Wagane Faye, *The Casamance Separatism: From Independence Claim to Resource Logic*, thesis, Monterey, Calif.: Naval Postgraduate School, June 2006, p. v.

the government realized all seven factors associated with strategic communication as a COIN approach in the final phase of the insurgency; see Chapter Three.) "In response, the MFDC [became] engaged in the illegal exploitation of [Senegal's] natural resources."[7] Ultimately, after dividing the insurgents through co-optation and amnesty, the government was able to settle with the majority of the insurgents, and the bandit activities of the remainder subsided to the level of a law-enforcement problem. At no point during this lengthy though relatively small and low-intensity insurgency was the government of Senegal ever seriously threatened.

### Turkey (PKK), 1984–1999

*Case Outcome: COIN Win*

The Kurdistan Workers' Party (PKK) began its insurgency as the outlawed party of an ethnic minority whose very existence was denied by the Turkish Constitution. The PKK struggled initially to develop support among a Kurdish population familiar with Turkish repression and not keen on further quixotic resistance. Over time, the PKK established itself as the premiere Kurdish cultural, political, and resistance organization and won significant regional popular support for its secessionist violence. This growth in support was a product not only of PKK successes but also of the repressive and heavy-handed response by Turkish authorities.

The PKK was defeated in 1999 after several years of "big stick" COIN by the Turks. Turkish forces had taken drastic measures to separate the insurgents from the population in the mountain villages in the area of conflict, aggressively pursued the insurgents into the mountains, sought to cut off cross-border support to them, and, most tellingly, made a political deal with extranational hosts to capture the authoritarian leader of the PKK, Abdullah Öcalan.

---

[7] Faye, 2006, p. v.

**Sudan (SPLA), 1984–2004**

*Case Outcome: COIN Loss*

The civil war in Sudan pitted the developed Arab Muslim government in the north against the Sudan People's Liberation Army (SPLA), representing Christians and animists in the rural, oil-rich south. The northern-based government sought to extend Islamic law throughout the country and benefit from the south's oil wealth while the southern rebels fought to obtain autonomy. An ineffective COIN strategy motivated by religious convictions and a "military-first" approach hampered the Sudanese government's attempts to crush the insurgency. Despite factionalism within the SPLA and changes in its external sources of support, the insurgents were able to continue to launch attacks on government forces and Sudan's oil pipelines and infrastructure in the south. After two decades of fighting and widespread famine, the government bowed to significant international pressure and agreed to a negotiated settlement with the SPLA that included a power-sharing agreement with the south and the promise of a referendum on secession.

**Uganda (ADF), 1986–2000**

*Case Outcome: COIN Win*

The Allied Democratic Forces (ADF) launched an insurgency against the Ugandan government in 1986, undertaking brutal attacks on civilians in the western region of the country. While a nominally Muslim group, the ADF did not have a clear religious agenda. Its vaguely stated goals were to overthrow the government and rid Uganda of Rwandan Tutsis. ADF attacks against civilians and military outposts increased in 1998, aided by external support from the Democratic Republic of the Congo (DRC) and Sudan. Initially, the Ugandan government was unable to maintain security in the region, but it eventually contained the insurgency by attacking the ADF's rear bases in the DRC and by developing special COIN units trained in mountain warfare.

**Papua New Guinea, 1988–1998**

*Case Outcome: COIN Loss*

The insurgency on the island of Bougainville in Papua New Guinea was sparked by protests by local landowners against the policies of outside mining companies. The protests became increasingly violent after the government sent in troops to defend the mines, leading to the evolution of a wider secessionist movement. Attempts by the Papua New Guinea army to crush the rebellion by employing local militia forces and instituting a military and economic blockade of the island failed. After six years of low-intensity conflict, the president of Papua New Guinea contracted with a private military firm to aid his COIN efforts. This decision led to the collapse of the government and a decline in public support for the military effort. Political negotiations were then pursued, leading to agreement on a cease-fire in 1998 that promised broad powers of self-governance for Bougainville.

**Liberia, 1989–1997**

*Case Outcome: COIN Loss*

What began as a civil war soon descended into a frenzy of violence, with as many as seven armed insurgent groups vying for power simultaneously. Under the command of Samuel Doe, the Liberian army and its ethnic Krahn counterparts attacked other tribes seen as threatening Doe's power, specifically those in Nimba County. In response, Charles Taylor organized a rebel force across the border in Côte d'Ivoire, where the insurgents organized, trained, and prepared for battle.

Soldiers from the Economic Community of West African States (ECOWAS), the ECOWAS Monitoring Group (ECOMOG), supplanted a deteriorating government as the primary COIN force. Atrocities were committed by all sides, including the COIN forces, as each side sought to gain control over valuable natural resources, such as diamonds, gold, iron ore, and timber. Accusations of brutality, collusion, and corruption, especially among the Nigerian contingent, plagued the COIN force throughout the conflict and certainly contributed to its dearth of credibility. With the civilian population suffering from war fatigue and the combatants themselves battle-weary, the fighting began to ebb. After 13 failed attempts to reach a peace agreement, the conflict was finally terminated when Taylor's National Patriotic Front of Liberia (NPFL) received the tacit approval of Nigeria to sit for elections. Receiving an overwhelming 75 percent of the vote, Taylor and his National Patriotic Party defeated the 12 other candidates contesting for power in an election marred by widespread voter intimidation.

### Rwanda, 1990–1994

*Case Outcome: COIN Loss*

The civil war in Rwanda began in 1990 when the Tutsi-dominated Rwandan Patriotic Front (RPF) invaded the country from its base in Uganda, seeking to establish democracy and the right of return for Tutsi refugees. After the RPF was turned back by Rwandan and French forces, it conducted an effective guerrilla campaign that ultimately led to the negotiation of a power-sharing agreement with the Hutu-led government. The political agreement with the RPF raised fears among the Hutu population over a reassertion of Tutsi power, however. In 1994, tensions came to a head when the plane carrying the Rwandan president was shot down and a genocidal campaign was declared by the radical Hutus, who gained control of the provisional government. Over the next few months, the government became preoccupied with eliminating Tutsis and moderate Hutus. French forces withheld direct military support, which allowed the RPF to regroup and quickly defeat the Rwandan army, gaining control of the capital with little opposition.

### Moldova, 1990–1992

*Case Outcome: COIN Loss*

Situated at the ethnic crossroads of several former empires, Moldova was host to violence that pitted pro-Romanian ethnic Moldovans against pro-Russian Dniesters in the early 1990s.[8] Suspicious that ethnic Moldovans in the government were planning to unite Moldova with Romania following independence, various elements in the Trans-dniester region along the Moldova-Ukraine border agitated for attacks against the Moldovan police. COIN forces were woefully underequipped and lacked a full-spectrum force. Furthermore, they were incapable of conducting high-intensity tactical assaults, despite having air supremacy and artillery superiority. The insurgents, on the other

---

[8] Moldova lies at the "ethnic crossroads" of greater Bessarabia, the intersection of German, Russian, Turkic, Romanian, and Ukrainian populations, history, and culture.

hand, acquired arms and heavy weapons from the Russian 14th Army, which was stationed in the region and provided seemingly unending tangible support to its ethnic kin. The support of a professional military proved to be the decisive factor in this lopsided insurgency.

The Moldovan government tried relentlessly and to no avail to solve the conflict through diplomacy, with the Moldovan leader Mircea Snegur unwilling to unleash the full fury of his COIN force against his enemies. The insurgents then defeated the COIN forces in a short but bloody battle with the assistance of the Russian 14th Army and various mercenaries. The Transdniester region retains de facto independence and is still under supervision by the Organization for Security and Co-Operation in Europe.

### Sierra Leone, 1991–2002

*Case Outcome: COIN Win*

The COIN force in this conflict comprised a series of actors and lasted for more than a decade. The insurgents terrorized the population through looting, rape, mutilation, and murder. Control of the diamond fields was a central focus of the conflict and served as the primary motivation for the insurgents. Money gained from the sale of diamonds was used to pay fighters and acquire sophisticated weaponry.

During one stage in the conflict, the government of Valentine Strasser and the National Provisional Ruling Council (NPRC) hired the South African mercenary firm Executive Outcomes (EO) to conduct COIN operations. Ultimately, British-led COIN forces adopted good COIN practices, quelled the fighting, and restored order to the country. Indeed, the lack of continuity between COIN forces—the Sierra Leonean army, EO, ECOMOG, and the UN Mission in Sierra Leone (UNAMSIL)—certainly contributed to the prolonged nature of the insurgency. However, by reorganizing UNAMSIL into a more modern force with new leadership and better coordination at all levels, the COIN force was eventually able to adopt positive COIN practices in the later stages of the conflict. In addition to acquiring helicopter gunships, deploying a full signals battalion, and using detailed maps and satellite imagery, the COIN force was able to maintain regular contact for the first time between troop-contributing countries, the

UN Security Council, and the secretariat through the UN's Department of Peacekeeping Operations. Furthermore, the COIN force kept its promise to protect the citizens during elections, providing the security necessary for Sierra Leoneans to vote at the polls with little fear of being attacked. Approximately 47,000 excombatants turned in their weapons, making the use of force by the counterinsurgents largely unnecessary during the final phase of the insurgency and lending a sense of credibility to the nearly disgraced UNAMSIL mission.

Some have called UNAMSIL the "model mission." To be sure, the COIN force was not without its shortcomings. However, at its height, UNAMSIL had roughly 17,000 troops and a large civilian staff operating at a cost of $700 million per year. Although not recognized as such at the time, adherence to strategic communication principles was a major factor in the mission's success. Indeed, the COIN force was able to maintain credibility with the local population, achieve unity of effort, and keep consistency in its message. This was accomplished by coordinating a large-scale disarmament program, successfully organizing elections, and, above all, providing a secure environment for the population.[9] These factors ultimately converged to allow the COIN force to prevail. In the 2002 elections, government- and COIN force–backed President Tejan Kabbah won the election while the insurgent-supported Revolutionary United Front Party failed to win a single seat.

### Algeria (GIA), 1992–2004

*Case Outcome: COIN Win*

The insurgency by the Armed Islamic Group (GIA) was prompted by the Algerian government's decision to cancel an election that was expected to put an Islamic party in power. The GIA initiated an urban terror campaign that became increasingly violent and targeted toward civilians. Although the military government in Algiers took brutal repressive actions against the insurgency, the GIA's attacks were viewed as even more violent and threatening. After a series of civilian massacres, by 1998, the GIA had lost much of its public support. The

---

[9] Funmi Olonisakin, *Peacekeeping in Sierra Leone: The Story of UNAMSIL*, Boulder, Colo.: Lynne Rienner Publishers, 2008, p. 111.

government then pursued a more effective COIN strategy, implementing an amnesty program, targeting the GIA hardliners, and offering political concessions, which helped to defeat an already weakened and fragmented GIA.

### Croatia, 1992–1995

*Case Outcome: COIN Win*

The insurgency in Croatia was fought between the Croatian army (HV) and various elements of the Yugoslav People's Army (JNA) and other Serb insurgent forces, which attempted to form their own independent enclave within Croatia known as the Republic of Serbian Krajina.

This three-year conflict saw innumerable failed cease-fires and egregious human rights violations committed by both sides. After two-and-a-half years of on-again, off-again fighting, the government prevailed as a result of two overarching factors: First, the Croatian military completely revamped itself from a second-rate fighting force into a formidable army with the assistance of the United States. Second, and equally important, the insurgents were abandoned by Belgrade as Serbian leader Slobodan Milosevic diverted his support elsewhere in the Balkans in an attempt to capitalize on insurgent success in neighboring Bosnia.

Following its transformation into a respected military, the HV was able to reduce tangible support to the insurgents and was strong enough to force the Serbs to fight as guerrillas. As a result, the government in Zagreb soon gained a reputation as a competent and capable state. While the Croats fought valiantly throughout the conflict, it was not until the final phase that they were able to put all the pieces together, launching two devastating COIN operations (Flash and Storm in May and August 1995, respectively).

Despite employing many poor COIN practices, including severe repression, the Croats exhibited enough positive practices on balance to prevail and secure the country's independence with its capital in Zagreb.

**Afghanistan (Post-Soviet), 1992–1996**

*Case Outcome: COIN Loss (Mixed, Favoring Insurgents)*

After the fall of the Soviet-supported Najibullah regime in 1992, Afghanistan lacked a legitimate central government. Kabul was governed by a coalition of former mujahadeen who competed for power among themselves, leading the country to devolve into a state of warlordism. The Taliban rose to prominence in 1994 by establishing a devout and disciplined militia that promised to restore order and security to the country. Taliban leaders received support from Pakistan and the war-weary Afghan population and were able to defeat what remained of the divided mujahadeen government, seize control of Kabul, and establish their own unified yet brutal government.

**Tajikistan, 1992–1997**

*Case Outcome: COIN Loss (Mixed, Favoring Insurgents)*

Less than a year after gaining independence from the Soviet Union, a mix of democrats, Tajik nationalists, and Islamists joined together to form the United Tajik Opposition (UTO) to challenge the communist-based government in Dushanbe. The UTO briefly gained control of the capital before being forced out by former government leaders, aided by Russian and Uzbek forces, employing brutal methods and inflicting significant civilian casualties. Upon its retreat, the UTO began launching attacks from bases in Afghanistan and became more closely associated with the Islamic movement.

The new government of Tajikistan subsequently did little to meet the needs of its populace and relied increasingly on Russian military support. While Tajik leader Emomali Rahmonov bowed to pressure to make some changes to his government and military leadership, they were not sufficient for the rebels, who continued to launch attacks. Only after the Taliban gained control of Afghanistan did Russia and Uzbekistan force the Tajik government to make greater concessions. This outside pressure led to the signing of the Peace and National Reconciliation Accord that met most of the UTO's political demands.

### Georgia/Abkhazia, 1992–1994

*Case Outcome: COIN Loss (Mixed, Favoring Insurgents)*

Long a hotbed of unrest, the disputed Abkhaz region was one of many areas that erupted in violence following the dissolution of the Soviet Union. The Georgia/Abkhazia border region became host to an insurgency after the kidnapping of Georgian government officials in 1992. Control of the capital, Sukhumi, switched hands several times, and the two-year conflict featured numerous failed cease-fires. Georgian COIN forces were defeated by Abkhazian insurgents in a conflict characterized by atrocities on both sides, which fits the general pattern of insurgency warfare in the post-Soviet Transcaucasus. The insurgent force was supplemented by volunteers from the Confederation of Peoples of the North Caucasus as well as Russian soldiers. The COIN force's inability to seal the country's borders allowed insurgent fighters, weapons, and materiel to prolong the conflict and provided the Abkhaz with the resources necessary to emerge victorious.

In addition to fighting Abkhaz insurgents, Georgian COIN forces were simultaneously engaged in a civil war against Georgian rebels and a war in South Ossetia. Ultimately, Russian soldiers tipped the balance in favor of the insurgents. Eager to end the fighting, Georgia begrudgingly accepted membership in the Commonwealth of Independent States as a precondition to Moscow's influence in bringing intra-Georgian fighting to a halt. Abkhazia gained de facto independence following the end of the insurgency and expelled the majority of the Georgian population living within its borders.

### Nagorno-Karabakh, 1992–1994

*Case Outcome: COIN Loss (Mixed, Favoring Insurgents)*

In another case of post-Soviet separatism, Azerbaijani authorities had governed Nagorno-Karabakh[10] directly with tacit approval from the Kremlin beginning in the late 1980s. When its Armenian majority declared the territory an independent state completely free from Azerbaijani rule, the two sides mobilized for war.

---

[10] Sometimes referred to in the literature as Nagorny-Karabagh or simply Qarabagh.

A more disciplined, better organized Karabakh Armenian insurgency defeated Azerbaijani COIN forces with the assistance of Russia, which provided weapons and troops to both sides in the conflict at various points. Political discord in Baku contributed significantly to the counterinsurgents' inability to muster an organized fighting force capable of defeating the insurgency. This case is a clear example of how ineffectual political leadership can adversely affect battlefield performance. Moreover, the Armenians possessed superior fighting skills from their experience in the former Soviet army. By the time the fighting came to an end, Armenian insurgents controlled not only Nagorno-Karabakh proper but also approximately 15 percent of Azerbaijani territory. Russia helped negotiate a cease-fire in May 1994, with a major stipulation being the recognition of Nagorno-Karabakh as a third party in the war. The situation in Nagorno-Karabakh remains unresolved today and is commonly referred to as a "frozen conflict" because of the inability to find a lasting resolution that is acceptable to all sides.

### Bosnia, 1992–1995

*Case Outcome: COIN Loss (Mixed, Favoring Insurgents)*

Following Bosnia's independence after the breakup of Yugoslavia, Bosnian Serb insurgents battled both Bosnian Muslims and Bosnian Croats for control of territory. COIN forces were underequipped and frequently fought with each other, while the insurgents were more organized, highly motivated, and better equipped. "Arkan's Tigers" were an extremely brutal but highly effective paramilitary unit operating throughout the country during the course of the insurgency. Bosnia was also the scene of the Srebrenica massacre, a campaign of ethnic cleansing orchestrated by Bosnian Serb insurgents that led to the deaths of more than 8,000 Bosnian Muslims and the exodus of an additional 25,000–30,000 refugees.

The Srebrenica massacre and another large-scale slaughter of civilians in Markale prompted the North Atlantic Treaty Organization (NATO) to intervene to end the fighting in the waning stages of the conflict, but Bosnian Serb insurgents secured a significant portion of territory and established the autonomous Republika Srpska, with close ties to Belgrade. The insurgency officially ended with the signing of the General Framework Agreement for Peace in Bosnia and Herzegovina in Paris on December 14, 1995.

### Burundi, 1993–2003

*Case Outcome: COIN Loss (Mixed, Favoring Insurgents)*

Burundi has long been plagued by ethnic conflict between the Tutsi minority, which maintained control of the government, and the majority Hutu population. In 1993, a series of ethnic massacres occurred after the country's first democratically elected Hutu president was assassinated. Subsequent instability led the Tutsi-dominated army to reassert control and reinstall a Tutsi-led government under Pierre Buyoya. The Buyoya regime implemented harsh COIN tactics, including widespread forcible resettlements, which served to reduce popular support for the government. Only after a decade of fighting, tens of thousands of deaths, and hundreds of thousands of displacements was a peace agreement finally reached with the Forces for the Defense of Democracy (FDD, one of the two major Hutu insurgent groups), in which the FDD agreed to abandon its armed struggle in exchange for guaranteed representation in the government.

### Chechnya I, 1994–1996

*Case Outcome: COIN Loss (Mixed, Favoring Insurgents)*

After failing to put down a rebellion by proxy in the breakaway Republic of Chechnya, Russian forces entered Grozny in December 1994. As the COIN force, the Russian army was plagued by a lack of training, severely disjointed command and control, and an unclear mission. Chechen insurgents, however, were highly motivated, familiar with the terrain, and able to marshal the resources necessary to exploit the Russians in asymmetric engagements.

The insurgents proved to be as adaptable and flexible as the COIN force was cumbersome. Realizing that hit-and-run tactics would require a high degree of mobility, the Chechens used light and portable grenade launchers, machine guns, and antitank weapons. The Chechens employed a technique known as "hugging," in which they stayed close to the Russian infantry in urban areas (they were usually less than 50 meters away) to reduce casualties from COIN artillery and air attacks. Furthermore, the insurgents had an extensive support network among the population, which provided them with real-time intelligence, food, weapons, and fuel. The conflict devolved into carnage with widespread atrocities committed by both sides before a Russian withdrawal in 1996.

**Afghanistan (Taliban), 1996–2001**

*Case Outcome: COIN Loss*

The Taliban took power from an unstable mujahadeen government in Kabul in 1996 and consolidated control over much of the country over the course of the next two years (with the help of Pakistani and foreign jihadist fighters). It failed, however, to establish an effective administrative apparatus that could provide services to the population or gain popular support for the regime. Welcomed at first for imposing order after years of chaos and bloodshed, the Taliban alienated many Afghanis and isolated itself from the international community with its brutal imposition of Islamic law. Ultimately, the Taliban's decision to host Osama bin Laden and allow him to establish al Qaeda training camps in Afghanistan led the Taliban to be driven from power by a U.S.-led coalition in November 2001.

**Zaire (Anti-Mobutu), 1996–1997**

*Case Outcome: COIN Loss*

The eastern region of Zaire was destabilized by the civil war in neighboring Rwanda and the influx of Hutus across the border. The displaced Hutus threatened the native Tutsi population in Zaire and established a base for rebel attacks against the new Rwandan government. In response to this threat, local Tutsis and the Rwandan army launched a preemptive attack on the Hutu militia and the Zairian army that supported it. A national rebel group under the leadership of Laurent Kabila was then formed to lead the fight against Zairian President Mobutu Sese Seko's regime. Kabila faced little resistance from Mobutu's poorly equipped army. Aided by the Rwandan, Ugandan, and Angolan armies, Kabila was able to take control of the capital within a matter of months.

### Kosovo, 1996–1999

*Case Outcome: COIN Loss*

Kosovo Liberation Army (KLA) insurgents battled Federal Republic of Yugoslavia COIN forces to a stalemate for most of the duration of this conflict. The KLA received financial assistance from the Kosovar Albanian diaspora and also benefited from the implosion of the government in neighboring Albania, which resulted in significant amounts of weaponry flooding across the border into the hands of the KLA.

The Racak massacre carried out by COIN forces prompted NATO to intervene on the side of the insurgents in an attempt to prevent ethnic cleansing and defeat the Milosevic regime. NATO forces conducted a three-month air campaign while KLA insurgents fought Serbian troops on the ground, resulting in Milosevic's capitulation and the imposition of a UN-backed peacekeeping force. While various commentators speculate on the motives for Milosevic's concession of the war, the primary reason is unequivocal: NATO airpower was *the* deciding factor in bringing the conflict to a close. Following its unilateral declaration of independence in February 2008 as the Republic of Kosovo, the country is recognized as an independent nation by 63 UN member states, including the United States.

### Nepal, 1997–2006

*Case Outcome: Coin Loss*

A democracy since 1990, Nepal fell prey to problems common to nascent democracies: corruption, excessive interparty politicking, and general paralysis and ineffectiveness.[11] This left the citizenry very open to the criticism offered by Maoist insurgents beginning in 1996. The insurgents' criticism of the state was further validated by the ineffective yet brutal COIN campaign launched by local police, which targeted both the insurgents and civilians. The one government institution with any kind of legitimacy, the monarchy, was shattered in a 2001 regicide. That same year, Nepal's army was unleashed on the insurgents for the first time and proved no more effective than the police had been.

---

[11] Thomas A. Marks, *Insurgency in Nepal*, Carlisle, Pa.: Strategic Studies Institute, U.S. Army War College, December 2003, p. 4.

Largely a ceremonial force, though substantially better equipped than the police or insurgents, the army made no headway against the Maoists and could not provide security for itself, let alone the larger population. King Gyanendra's 2005 royalist seizure of the government cast much of Nepali civil society into opposition. The Maoist insurgents opportunistically joined with a prodemocracy coalition and secured a significant place for themselves in the new government after the combination of military and civil pressure forced the king to capitulate in 2006.

#### Democratic Republic of the Congo (Anti-Kabila), 1998–2003

*Case Outcome: COIN Loss (Mixed, Favoring Insurgents)*

The second Congolese war began in 1998 with the invasion of Rwandan and Ugandan forces seeking to overthrow DRC President Laurent Kabila, their former ally. Kabila countered the threat to his government by engaging Angolan, Zimbabwean, and Namibian forces and local militia groups in his defense. The war then devolved into a conflict of pillage and partition as the various regional forces battled for control of the country's resources. Efforts toward political compromise and international negotiation began in 2001 after the president was assassinated and replaced by his son, Joseph. Joseph Kabila eventually concluded a cease-fire agreement with the Ugandan, Rwandan, and other foreign forces and a power-sharing deal with the major rebel groups, which greatly reduced the level of fighting by 2003.

## Case Narrative Results

These narratives provide some context for the quantitative analysis presented in the next chapter. The accompanying volume contains more detail for each case, including

- a short summary of the case
- a summary of each phase of the case, including key factors for that phase

- a discussion of the conventional explanations for the outcomes of the case, as offered in existing secondary analysis
- a list of distinct features of the case.

Beyond this, we offer no separate analysis of the individual cases; all of the analyses are of aggregate-level data across all of the cases together. In fact, one of our most striking findings is that we do not need to discuss any of the distinct features or unique narrative peculiarities of the individual cases to wholly explain the outcomes: The patterns of presence or absence of factors common to all of the cases are sufficient to explain all of the outcomes (see Chapter Four). In fact, our analysis supports the idea that it can be a mistake to learn too many "lessons" from a single case, as the peculiarities and distinctions of a single case may obfuscate otherwise critical and enduring relationships between COIN practices and outcomes.

CHAPTER THREE

# Testing the Approaches to Counterinsurgency

Insurgency is a complex subset of warfare. Current U.S. doctrine defines *insurgency* as "the organized use of subversion or violence by a group or movement that seeks to overthrow or force change of a governing authority."[1] Essentially, insurgency is an organized, protracted politico-military struggle designed to weaken the control and legitimacy of an established government, occupying power, or other political authority while increasing insurgent control.

The mirror image of insurgency is counterinsurgency, a combination of offensive, defensive, and stability operations. *Counterinsurgency* is defined as "comprehensive civilian and military efforts taken to defeat an insurgency and to address any core grievances."[2]

Our review of the COIN literature covered everything from the classics to contemporary contributions from academics, practitioners, and military officers. We also looked (though with less intensity) at the literature on strategies for insurgents. Based on this broad review, we extrapolated 20 distinct approaches, partial approaches, or collections of practical advice for COIN (or insurgency). This chapter tests these 20 approaches against the historical record of our 30 cases. We find strong empirical evidence supporting 13 of these approaches and strong evidence against three.

---

[1] U.S. Joint Chiefs of Staff, *Dictionary of Military and Associated Terms*, Joint Publication 1-02, Washington, D.C., April 21, 2001, as amended through October 31, 2009, p. 266.

[2] U.S. Joint Chiefs of Staff, 2001, p. 128.

The 20 COIN approaches are listed in Table 3.1. To impose some order on the identified approaches, we have grouped them loosely into three categories: classic COIN approaches, contemporary COIN approaches, and insurgent approaches. Many classic approaches are still prominently advocated in contemporary discourse, so the label "classic" is in no way intended to suggest that they are dated. Similarly, most of the contemporary approaches have classical roots. Within the broader classic and contemporary categories, approaches are arranged such that we begin with those that are more firmly aligned with population-centered COIN theory and progress to those more closely aligned with insurgent-centered theory.

**Table 3.1**
**Twenty Approaches to COIN Tested in This Research**

| Category | Approach |
|---|---|
| Classic COIN approaches | Development (classic "hearts and minds") |
| | Pacification |
| | Legitimacy |
| | Democracy |
| | Resettlement |
| | Cost-benefit |
| | Border control |
| | "Crush them" |
| | Amnesty/rewards |
| Contemporary COIN approaches | Strategic communication |
| | Field Manual (FM) 3-24, *Counterinsurgency* |
| | "Beat cop" |
| | "Boots on the ground" |
| | "Put a local face on it" |
| | Cultural awareness |
| | Tangible support reduction |
| | Criticality of intelligence |
| | Flexibility and adaptability |
| Insurgent approaches | Insurgent support strategies |
| | Continuation and contestation |

## Representing the Approaches in the Data

As we reviewed and synthesized the approaches, we identified a set of core tenets of each approach (reported later in this chapter). Based on these tenets, we then identified sets of discrete, measurable factors to represent each approach and identified them as either present or absent in each case. Details of the process that we used to select and refine the factors, along with details of the process by which the factors were determined to be present or absent for each case, can be found in Appendix A, in the section "Factor Generation, Evaluation, and Scoring."

### Analysis of the Relationships Between Case Factors and Case Outcomes

Preliminary analyses involved the comparison of the relationships between different factors and the case outcomes. This began with the assessment of simple 2×2 tables for each factor against each outcome. Table 3.2 is a sample of such a table.

Table 3.2 divides the 30 cases by their values on case outcome (either COIN loss or COIN win) and value on COIN force credibility (either present or absent). Adding up all four cells in the table gives a sum of 30, the number of cases. The sum of the cells in the first column is 22, the total number of COIN losses; the sum of the cells in the second column is eight, the total number of COIN wins.

**Table 3.2**
**Sample 2×2 Table: COIN Force Credibility Versus Case Outcome**

| | | Case Outcome | |
|---|---|---|---|
| | | **COIN Loss** | **COIN Win** |
| COIN force maintained credibility with population in area of conflict (includes expectation management) | **1 (present)** | 0 | 5 |
| | **0 (absent)** | 22 | 3 |

Summing by row, we see that in five cases COIN force credibility was present and in 25 cases it was absent. Table 3.2 shows a strong relationship between COIN force credibility and case outcome. In every case in which COIN force credibility was present during the decisive phase (five cases), the COIN force won.

### Factor Stacks

Each approach is represented by between one and 10 discrete factors. The factors are listed after the tenets for each approach later in this chapter. Because each approach is represented by more than one factor, we faced a challenging question: How many of the factors associated with a given approach to COIN must have been present in a case before the COIN force is considered to have applied that approach? Rather than attempting to answer this question in an abstract or theory-based way, we let the data speak and sought the best empirical cut point for each approach.

For each COIN approach, we created a new factor that was the sum of all the factors tied to that approach and present in a given phase or case. We then chose a threshold value for that sum that maximized the number of COIN wins associated with the approach and minimized the number of COIN losses. Here is a concrete example: Strategic communication as a COIN approach is represented in the data by seven discrete factors (listed later in this chapter in the section "Strategic Communication"). For each case, we summed these seven factors, creating a new variable, "sum of strategic communication factors." The results are shown in Table 3.3.

Here, the empirical cut point is clearly at two or more. Having at least two strategic communication factors captures all eight COIN wins and excludes all but two COIN losses. Thus, we created a single factor to represent strategic communication in the analysis: "at least two strategic communication factors," which was evaluated as present or absent in each phase of each case, just like all the other factors in the analysis. We created a "factor stack" to represent each of the 20 approaches we tested. A more detailed discussion of factor stacks can be found in Appendix A in the section "Factor Stacks"; possible shortcomings of this approach are discussed in Appendix C.

**Table 3.3**
**Sum of Strategic Communication Factors Versus Case Outcome (empirical cut point in red)**

| Sum of strategic communication factors | Case Outcome: COIN Loss | Case Outcome: COIN Win |
|---|---|---|
| 7 | 0 | 1 |
| 6 | 0 | 2 |
| 5 | 0 | 1 |
| 4 | 0 | 0 |
| 3 | 1 | 4 |
| 2 | 1 | 4 |
| 1 | 5 | 0 |
| 0 | 15 | 0 |

## Tests of Each Approach

In this section, we introduce and test each of the COIN approaches listed in Table 3.1. Each entry follows the following format: The approach is introduced and the core tenets of that approach as identified in the literature are presented as a bulleted list. This is followed by a list of the specific factors chosen to represent the approach in the analysis and measured as present or absent in each phase of each case. Next is a discussion of the threshold for the factor stack chosen to represent the approach as a single factor. A table shows the relationship between the approach and the outcome, and a summary assessment of the empirical support for the approach is levied. These assessments indicate whether the approach received strong support from the evidence in our analysis, received some support from the evidence, received strong evidence against, or could not be tested. Strength of support is based on the ability of the approach (by way of its factor stack) to predict or discriminate between case outcomes. Approaches were considered to have strong support if the bivariate relationship between the approach's factor stack and the outcome was very strong (i.e., using it and it alone is a very strong indicator of the outcome), some support if there was a moderately strong correlation between the approach's factor stack and the outcome but the approach's application occurred in a significant number of COIN losses,[3] strong evidence against if the approach's application predicted a greater proportion of losses than wins, and untestable if the approach was never used.[4]

### Classic COIN Approaches

**Development (Classic "Hearts and Minds").** The "hearts and minds"[5] approach to COIN should perhaps more properly be called the "development" approach. Core tenets are as follows:

- Development leads to indigenous support.
- Those who have something worth fighting for will fight for it.
- Development leads to increased indigenous capacity.
- Development is painful; short-term handouts ease the pain of development.

While the phrase *hearts and minds* itself may have become a cliché, the ideas behind this approach still retain relevance. The central proposition is that development and modernity will give the population a positive stake in order and good governance and thus deprive insurgents of their support. The catch, of course, is that development and modernity can cause painful dislocations and disruptions in the old institutions of a traditional society.[6] The solution, then, "is therefore to win the public's support for the government by ameliorating

---

[3] In this analysis, the threshold for "moderately strong" is a bivariate correlation of 0.5.

[4] Two of the approaches, "put a local face on it" and cultural awareness, are supporting approaches that are applicable only when the primary COIN force is an external force. The primary COIN force was composed of outsiders in only three of the 30 cases in our analysis; the factors for "put a local face on it" and cultural awareness were present in none of these cases. There is thus insufficient evidence to test these two approaches in any way.

[5] The phrase *hearts and minds* can be traced to Sir Gerald Templer, who used it to describe aspects of the British COIN campaign in Malaya (1948–1960).

[6] This idea is articulated thoroughly in Samuel Huntington, *Political Order in Changing Societies*, New Haven, Conn.: Yale University Press, 1968.

some of the negative effects of development while speeding up the provision of modernity's benefits."[7] Furthermore, this approach has suffered from the "chicken-and-egg" dilemma of what should come first, security or development. As evidenced by the contemporary insurgencies in Iraq and Afghanistan, no clear-cut answer to this question has been realized.

This approach to COIN prescribes increasing political rights, improving standards of living, and reducing corruption in government while pursuing a path to development. The development approach follows popular support–based theory, positing that development leads to support and support leads to positive COIN outcomes.[8] Extra nuance comes in with the proposed relationships between development and indigenous capacity on the one hand and the inclination to resist insurgents on the other.

While called "hearts and minds" at its inception, there is very little in this approach that pertains to influence or the way the phrase is used (or misused) in the contemporary era.

The development approach is represented in our analysis by two factors, both of which needed to be present for a COIN force to receive credit for employing this approach:

- Short-term investments, improvements in infrastructure or development, or property reform occurred in the area of conflict that was controlled or claimed by the COIN force.
- In the area of conflict, the COIN force was *not* perceived as worse than the insurgents.

As Table 3.4 shows, both factors appear in four of the eight cases in which the COIN force won and in none of the losses. Since the

---

7 Long, 2006, p. x.

8 Long, 2006, pp. 21–23; David C. Gompert, John Gordon IV, David R. Frelinger, Seth G. Jones, Martin C. Libicki, Edward O'Connell, Brooke Stearns Lawson, and Robert E. Hunter, *War by Other Means: Building Complete and Balanced Capabilities for Counterinsurgency: RAND Counterinsurgency Study—Final Report*, Santa Monica, Calif.: RAND Corporation, MG-595/2-OSD, 2008, pp. 91–92.

**Table 3.4**
**Both Development Factors Versus Case Outcome**

| | | Case Outcome: COIN Loss | Case Outcome: COIN Win |
|---|---|---|---|
| Both development factors | Yes | 0 | 4 |
| | No | 22 | 4 |

COIN force wins every time it adheres to this approach, *development receives strong support in our analysis.*

The four cases whose decisive phase included both development factors are El Salvador, Senegal, Peru, and Sierra Leone.

**Pacification.** Primarily thought of as a Vietnam War–era approach, *pacification* is a broad and fairly vague umbrella term for a handful of population-centric COIN approaches that focus on the local level.[9] These approaches emphasize development and security, hand in hand, in initially small but then expanding locales. Classic pacification relates to the "community policing" perspective that was developed domestically in the United States in the 1970s.[10]

The core tenets of pacification are as follows:

- "All politics is local."[11]
- Engage in or enable community policing or beat-cop activities.[12]

---

[9] Long, 2006, p. 52.

[10] Long, 2006, p. 53.

[11] "All Politics Is Local" is the heading of the section on pacification in Long, 2006, p. 52; the quote is attributed to former Speaker of the House Thomas P. "Tip" O'Neill, Jr.

[12] Long, 2006, p. 53. The phrase "beat-cop behaviors" can be found in David Kilcullen, "Twenty-Eight Articles: Fundamentals of Company-Level Counterinsurgency," *IO Sphere*, Summer 2006a, p. 29.

- Development and security need to go hand in hand; either without the other can be counterproductive.[13]

Again, while often considered an approach of yesteryear, pacification has stood the test of time, bridging the gap between classic and contemporary. This can be directly attributed to its focus on the population as a key to effective COIN. The support of the population is again implicitly important, but here that support is won through a local focus. A premium is placed on providing and maintaining security at the local community or village level and then expanding the area that is "pacified."

Pacification is represented by three factors in our analysis:

- A perception of security was created or maintained among populations in areas that the COIN force claimed to control.
- Short-term investments, improvements in infrastructure or development, or property reform occurred in the area of conflict that was controlled or claimed by the COIN force.
- The COIN force established and then expanded secure areas.

The empirical cut point for the factor stack leaves pacification represented by a single factor: "at least one pacification factor present."

*Pacification receives strong support from these data.* All eight COIN wins have at least one pacification factor, and only one of 22 losses does (the single loss was Afghanistan [Taliban]). Save for this single COIN loss, the application of the pacification approach perfectly predicts success. All five cases in which two or more of these factors were present are COIN wins. (See Table 3.5.)

---

[13] Long, 2006, p. 53. This thinking seems to have been adopted by COIN experts and U.S. government departments. See David Kilcullen, "Three Pillars of Counterinsurgency," presentation, U.S. Government Counterinsurgency Conference, Washington, D.C., September 28, 2006b. This theme has also been commandeered by the U.S. Department of State, as evidenced in a report released in October 2007 titled *Counterinsurgency for U.S. Government Policymakers: A Work in Progress.*

**Table 3.5**
**Number of Pacification Factors Present Versus Case Outcome**

| | | Case Outcome | |
|---|---|---|---|
| | | COIN Loss | COIN Win |
| Number of pacification factors | 3 | 0 | 2 |
| | 2 | 0 | 3 |
| | 1 | 1 | 3 |
| | 0 | 21 | 0 |

The individual factors for the pacification approach are very strong predictors (which is why the threshold for implementation of the approach is 1). "Perception of security created or maintained among population in areas COIN force claimed to control" appears in four cases, all of which are COIN wins. "Short-term investments, improvements in infrastructure/development, or property reform in area of conflict" is present in five cases, all of which are COIN wins. "COIN force established and then expanded secure areas" occurred in seven cases, six of which are COIN force wins.

**Legitimacy.** Sociologist Max Weber wrote extensively on the societal importance of legitimacy and authority.[14] Legitimacy is fundamentally a popular support–based approach. The core tenets are as follows:

- Insurgency is fundamentally a contest of legitimacy.[15]
- A legitimate government
  - has a monopoly on the use of violence[16]

---

[14] Max Weber, "Politics as a Vocation," in H. H. Gerth and C. Wright Mills, eds., *From Max Weber: Essays in Sociology*, New York: Oxford University Press, 1958, p. 78.

[15] Eliot Cohen, Conrad Crane, Jan Horvath, and John Nagl, "Principles, Imperatives, and Paradoxes of Counterinsurgency," *Military Review*, March–April 2006, p. 49.

[16] Max Weber defined the state as "a human community that (successfully) claims the monopoly of the legitimate use of physical force within a given territory" (Weber, 1958, p. 78).

   - maintains the rule of law[17]
   - is a provider of basic services.[18]
- The government's role can be expanded to include the need to protect legitimacy by avoiding collateral damage.[19]

This position asserts that people offer their support to the side that they perceive as having the greatest legitimacy. If made to appear illegitimate, the insurgency will lose support and supporters and wither away. If legitimacy accrues to the government, then the government will enjoy greater support, greater patience for its shortcomings, and better intelligence on insurgents. Consequently, if the government is seen as corrupt, self-serving, and inept, the population may be persuaded to support the insurgents, who, even if somewhat draconian in their rule, are perceived to be more just and fair than a puppet regime installed from outside.

Perceptions of legitimacy are complicated and involve contextual nuances. Legitimacy should always be evaluated as a perception of the stakeholders, not against some arbitrary external standard.

Because so many different aspects of and behaviors by the government and the COIN force can affect perceptions of legitimacy in a way that could relate to COIN outcomes, we divide legitimacy into "government legitimacy" and "legitimacy of force" for our analysis.

***Government Legitimacy.*** Government legitimacy was represented by the following five factors:

- Government corruption was reduced or good governance increased since the onset of the conflict.
- Government leaders were selected in a manner considered just and fair by the majority of the population in the area of conflict.

---

[17] Headquarters, U.S. Department of the Army, and Headquarters, U.S. Marine Corps, 2007, p. 154.

[18] Headquarters, U.S. Department of the Army, and Headquarters, U.S. Marine Corps, 2007, p. 153.

[19] Montgomery McFate and Andrea V. Jackson, "The Object Beyond War: Counterinsurgency and the Four Tools of Political Competition," *Military Review*, January–February 2006, pp. 14–16.

- The majority of citizens viewed the government as legitimate in the area of conflict.
- The government provided better governance than insurgents in the area of conflict.
- The COIN force provided or ensured the provision of basic services in areas that it controlled or claimed to control.

Having at least two of these factors was an empirical threshold; 10 cases had at least two government legitimacy factors, and seven of them were COIN wins and three were COIN losses. Thus, there is *strong evidence in support of the importance of government legitimacy.* (See Table 3.6.)

***Legitimate Use of Force.*** Five factors represent the legitimacy of the COIN forces' use of force:

- The COIN force avoided excessive collateral damage, disproportionate use of force, or other illegitimate applications of force.
- COIN force collateral damage was *not* perceived by the population in the area of conflict as worse than the insurgents'.
- In the area of conflict, the COIN force was *not* perceived as worse than the insurgents.

**Table 3.6**
**At Least Two Government Legitimacy Factors Versus Case Outcome**

| | | Case Outcome | |
|---|---|---|---|
| | | COIN Loss | COIN Win |
| At least two government legitimacy factors | Yes | 3 | 7 |
| | No | 17 | 1 |

- The perception of security was created or maintained among populations in areas that the COIN force claimed to control.
- The COIN force was *not* viewed as an occupying force in the area of conflict.

The empirical break point for legitimate use of force was three of the five factors. Six of eight COIN wins had at least three "legitimate use of force" factors, while only four of 22 losses did so. (See Table 3.7.) The two COIN victories that lacked legitimate use of force were Turkey and Croatia.

While this is a relatively strong correlation (~0.53), this factor stack applies to only 75 percent of COIN wins and covers a handful of losses, too. While *this evidence offers some support in favor of legitimate use of force*, it is clear that other approaches' factors are necessary for a complete explanation of an outcome.

Of the individual legitimate use of force factors, findings regarding the COIN forces' use of force relative to the insurgents' are interesting. First, for every case in which the COIN force avoided excessive collateral damage, disproportionate use of force, or other illegitimate applications of force, it won—but that occurred in only three cases. Both "COIN force collateral damage *not* perceived by population in area of conflict as worse than insurgents'" and "In area of conflict,

**Table 3.7**
**At Least Three Legitimate Use of Force Factors Versus Case Outcome**

| At least three legitimate use of force factors | | Case Outcome: COIN Loss | Case Outcome: COIN Win |
|---|---|---|---|
| | Yes | 4 | 6 |
| | No | 18 | 2 |

COIN force *not* perceived as worse than insurgents" occurred in the majority of COIN wins but also occurred in numerous COIN losses (nine and seven losses, respectively). This suggests that not being perceived as worse than the insurgents helps a COIN force but is a far cry from being sufficient.

**Democracy.** Democracy is advocated as a way to increase the legitimacy of a government and resolve grievances short of violence. The core tenets of this approach are as follows:[20]

- Democratic voice and expression resolve grievances.
- Democracy equals legitimacy.

At its undertheorized worst, democracy is held to be a panacea.[21] More reasonable articulations posit that democracy and democratization help resolve grievances through democratic expression, or they equate democracy with legitimacy.

Democracy is represented by four factors, the first two of which are mutually exclusive (so no more than three of the four factors could be present in any one case):

- The government is a functional democracy.
- The government is a partial or transitional democracy.
- Free and fair elections were held.
- The government respects human rights and allows a free press.

The empirical cut point is having at least one of these four factors. All eight COIN wins had at least one democracy factor, though seven COIN losses did too. (See Table 3.8.) By our criteria, this is *evidence of some support for democracy as a COIN approach*. However, because all

---

[20] Alhough this is certainly not the only example of this kind of thinking, both tenets can be found in Strategic Communication and Public Diplomacy Policy Coordinating Committee, *U.S. National Strategy for Public Diplomacy and Strategic Communication*, Washington, D.C., June 2007, p. 3.

[21] The word *democracy* appears 52 times in the 49-page 2006 *National Security Strategy of the United States of America*. The strategy has an entire chapter dedicated to the establishment and promotion of democracy, titled "Expand the Circle of Development by Opening Societies and Building the Infrastructure of Democracy."

**Table 3.8**
**At Least One Democracy Factor Versus Case Outcome**

| At least one democracy factor | Case Outcome: COIN Loss | Case Outcome: COIN Win |
|---|---|---|
| Yes | 7 | 8 |
| No | 15 | 0 |

eight wins had at least one democracy factor, we cannot rule it out as a necessary but insufficient contributor to COIN success. Indeed, it is one of the several things that all COIN winners have going for them and appears to be one of victory's "thousand fathers."

***Democratization in the Phases.*** As noted, all eight COIN wins had at least one democracy factor in their decisive phase. The phase-level data regarding democracy factors are also interesting. Looking at the phase data and at changes between phases, six of the eight COIN wins had at least one democracy factor go from absent to present at some point during the conflict; only one COIN loss had a democracy factor go from absent to present, and several losses had democracy factors go from present to absent. This strongly suggests that increasing democratization may be just as important for the resolution of insurgencies as democratic practices themselves.

**Resettlement ("Drain the Swamp").** *Pacification* is also the term sometimes applied to relocation and resettlement—actions that take the prescription to separate the population from the insurgents quite literally.[22]

---

[22] Kelly M. Greenhill, *Draining the Sea, or Feeding the Fire? The Use of Population Relocation in Counterinsurgency Operations*, Center for International Security and Cooperation, Stanford University, forthcoming.

This approach has also been referred to as "draining the swamp."[23] This version of draining the swamp has two tenets:

- The population is the sea in which the fish of insurgency swim.[24]
- Separate the insurgents from the population (physically, in this case).[25]

If the COIN force is unable to provide security to the population where it is and insurgents are extracting necessary inputs straight from that population, relocation of that population might seem to be an obvious solution. According to Kelly Greenhill's research, the historical record for this form of pacification is extremely poor.[26] Citing examples in Turkey, Burundi, Indonesia, and Colombia, Greenhill finds that relocations are likely to work only "in those rare cases where promises made by the counterinsurgents actually are fulfilled and the quality of life actually is improved for the displaced population—i.e., where a culture of cooperation and co-optation can be inculcated."[27] The oft-invoked example of success in this approach is the British in Malaya.[28] Other attempts were made by the British Army in the Boer War (1899–1902), the Spanish Army during the insurrection in

---

[23] This phrase is often attributed to former Secretary of Defense Donald Rumsfeld in remarks made shortly after the attacks of September 11, 2001. See "Rumsfeld: U.S. Must Drain the Swamp," CNN.com, September 19, 2001. It is also a common phrase for the strategy of separating insurgents from the population, often used by the British in past COIN campaigns. For more information, see Wade Markel, "Draining the Swamp: The British Strategy of Population Control," *Parameters*, Spring 2006, and Headquarters, U.S. Department of the Army, and Headquarters, U.S. Marine Corps, 2007, p. 180.

[24] Mao Tse-Tung, *On Guerrilla Warfare*, Samuel B. Griffith II, trans., New York: Praeger, 1961.

[25] Greenhill, forthcoming.

[26] Greenhill, forthcoming.

[27] Greenhill, forthcoming, p. 3.

[28] John Nagl, *Learning to Eat Soup with a Knife: Counterinsurgency Lessons from Malaya and Vietnam*, Chicago, Ill.: University of Chicago Press, 2005; Thomas E. Willis II, "Lessons from the Past: Successful British Counterinsurgency Operations in Malaya 1948–1960," *Infantry Magazine*, July–August 2005; Kalev I. Sepp, "Best Practices in Counterinsurgency," *Military Review*, May–June 2005.

Cuba (1895–1898), and the U.S. Army in the Philippines during the Spanish-American War (1898–1902).[29]

The focus here is on denying the adversary the support of the population. If the population cannot be secured in place (as the generic version of pacification obviously prefers), then it must be removed to a location where it can.

The resettlement approach is represented by a single factor in our analysis:

- The COIN force resettled or removed civilian populations for population control.

The astute reader will note that this factor alone does not capture the nuance of effective resettlement as implemented by the British in Malaya. In fact, in our preliminary data collection, we included an additional factor:

- Relocated populations were sufficiently compensated, and their quality of life improved.

However, this factor was not evaluated to be present in any phase of any case, so we removed the variable from the analysis. The omission of this part of the approach from its application in the cases is a costly one: While relocations occurred in the decisive phase of nine cases, the COIN force prevailed in only one of them (Turkey). (See Table 3.9.)

One could convincingly argue that in no case did the COIN force diligently attend to the needs of the relocated population, so we do not need to test it. However, nine COIN forces engaged in forced resettlement as an intentional part of their COIN strategies, declaredly following the principles of this approach. Just because they failed to employ all of the elements of the approach does not prevent us from concluding that *these data provide strong evidence against resettlement* as it has been applied in these cases. Declaring the approach untested in these

[29] Greenhill, forthcoming.

**Table 3.9**
**Resettlement Versus Case Outcome**

| Resettlement | | Case Outcome: COIN Loss | Case Outcome: COIN Win |
|---|---|---|---|
| Resettlement | Yes | 8 | 1 |
| | No | 14 | 7 |

data would send an ambiguous message, while the data unambiguously show that forced resettlement (by itself) is a poor COIN practice.

**Cost-Benefit.** During the Vietnam War era and writing in opposition to those who advocated popular support–based approaches to COIN, RAND's Nathan Constantin Leites and Charles Wolf, Jr., focused instead on insurgents' needs for certain inputs.[30] This insurgent-focused approach has the following tenets:[31]

- Treat the insurgency as a system.
- COIN forces must increase the cost of insurgent inputs.
- COIN forces must interrupt the process by which inputs are converted into activities.
- COIN forces must destroy insurgent outputs.
- COIN forces should seek to blunt the impact of insurgent outputs.

Leites and Wolf suggested that insurgencies are best viewed as systems and that COIN efforts should be evaluated in terms of how well they either raised the cost of inputs to the system or interfered

---

[30] Nathan Constantin Leites and Charles Wolf, Jr., *Rebellion and Authority: An Analytic Essay on Insurgent Conflicts*, Santa Monica, Calif: RAND Corporation, R-462-ARPA, 1970.

[31] Also referred to as "carrots and sticks." These tenets are found in Long, 2006, pp. 24–26.

with outputs.[32] This approach came to be known as "cost-benefit" and indicated that, under certain circumstances, "development" could lead to increased inputs for insurgents:

> In effect, development made more resources available to citizens, which insurgents could then acquire from the population through persuasion, coercion, or a combination of the two. Thus, paradoxically, programs designed to reduce popular support for insurgents could actually reduce the insurgent cost for inputs such as food.[33]

The approach relies on system dynamics theory to posit that disrupting the input or output of an insurgent system will result in a reduction of the overall impact of insurgent output.

The core elements of a cost-benefit approach are captured in six factors in this analysis:

- COIN force efforts resulted in increased costs for insurgent processes.
- COIN forces effectively disrupted insurgent recruiting.
- COIN forces effectively disrupted insurgent materiel acquisition.
- COIN forces effectively disrupted insurgent intelligence.
- COIN forces effectively disrupted insurgent financing.
- COIN forces effectively disrupted insurgent command and control.

Having at least two of these six factors is the empirical cut point used as the threshold for the factor stack to represent the cost-benefit approach. All eight of the COIN wins and only two COIN losses featured at least two cost-benefit factors. (See Table 3.10.) *This constitutes strong evidence in favor of cost-benefit.*

The six individual factors of the cost-benefit approach are all quite good predictors of COIN success by themselves. While none of them individually occurs in more than six of the COIN-winning cases (most

---

[32] Long, 2006, p. 25.

[33] Long, 2006, p. 25.

**Table 3.10**
**At Least Two Cost-Benefit Factors Versus Case Outcome**

| | | Case Outcome | |
|---|---|---|---|
| | | COIN Loss | COIN Win |
| At least two cost-benefit factors | Yes | 2 | 8 |
| | No | 20 | 0 |

occur in exactly four COIN wins), none of them occurs in more than one COIN loss.

**Border Control.** The importance of border security follows the logic of the cost-benefit approach; if the insurgent "system" is able to freely receive inputs from cross-border sources, efforts to restrict in-country insurgent inputs will be far less consequential. "Indeed, with few exceptions (perhaps most notably Cuba), successful insurgencies have been able to obtain aid and comfort from outside sources."[34] Tenets include the following:[35]

- Insurgencies benefit from cross-border support and havens.
- Securing the border reduces the flow of fighters and materiel and/or provides useful intelligence.
- Secure borders increase international legitimacy.

The importance of border security is clearly evident in Afghanistan, where the Taliban is able to move fighters, money, and materiel back and forth between that country and neighboring Pakistan. Although remotely piloted drones patrol the skies above the Feder-

[34] Long, 2006, p. 49.

[35] Long, 2006, pp. 49–51; Gompert et al., 2008, p. 190; also see Paul Staniland, "Defeating Transnational Insurgencies: The Best Offense Is a Good Fence," *Washington Quarterly*, Vol. 29, No. 1, Winter 2005–2006.

ally Administered Tribal Areas on the Pakistani side of the border, the rugged terrain and centuries-old smuggling routes make sealing the border virtually impossible.

Border control is a partial approach to COIN and connects to other approaches, such as cost-benefit (deprive the insurgents of cross-border inputs), tangible support reduction, and legitimacy.

Border control is represented in the analysis by a single factor:

- The flow of cross-border insurgent support significantly decreased or remained dramatically reduced or largely absent.

The presence of this factor is a strong predictor of COIN success: All eight COIN wins reduced or prevented the flow of insurgent support across borders in the decisive phase, while that occurred in only a single COIN loss. (See Table 3.11.) *This is strong evidence in support of border control as a COIN approach.*

**Table 3.11**
**Border Control Versus Case Outcome**

| | | Case Outcome | |
|---|---|---|---|
| | | COIN Loss | COIN Win |
| Flow of cross-border insurgent support decreased or absent | Yes | 1 | 8 |
| | No | 21 | 0 |

**"Crush Them."** James Clancy and Chuck Crosset suggest that, if diagnosed sufficiently early, a nascent insurgency can be annihilated through the vigorous application of force and repression. While Clancy and Crosset's version of this approach is intended to apply only to nascent insurgencies, "crush them" is also a more general approach to COIN that predates the modern era.[36] (Roman "decimation" can be seen as an early application of this approach.)

This position has but a single tenet:

- Escalating repression can crush an insurgency.

The approach sits uneasily alongside legitimacy and popular support–based approaches, as repression and unrestrained force are unlikely to be well regarded by the population at large. Indeed, an established insurgency met with escalating repression would likely gain further domestic and international support and legitimacy. What separates a nascent insurgency from a mature one and the resulting implications for this theory are not well articulated in the existing literature. The use of escalating repression is not limited strictly to dictatorships, but democracies typically lack the political will to employ this tactic for a prolonged period. After all, democracies, in theory at least, must respond to their domestic constituencies, while dictatorships have far more leeway in crafting COIN strategies.

Escalating repression as a COIN approach is captured in the analysis by two factors:

- The COIN force employed escalating repression.
- The COIN force employed collective punishment.

Our data provide *strong evidence against repression as an approach to COIN*, as fully 18 of 22 COIN losses recorded the presence of both of these factors and only two COIN-winning cases did so (Turkey and Croatia). (See Table 3.12.) Using repression does not guarantee defeat (two winning COIN forces employed both repressive approaches, and a third engaged in one), but it is unambiguously a poor approach.

---

[36] James Clancy and Chuck Crosset, "Measuring Effectiveness in Irregular Warfare," *Parameters*, Summer 2007. The authors note that "combat operations have defeated insurgencies by overwhelming and annihilating the insurgency and its supporters through bombings, massive raids, heavy shelling, and even torture and executions" (p. 91). "The quick and overwhelming smothering of an infant insurgency is a very effective tactic" (p. 92).

**Table 3.12**
**Both "Crush Them" Factors Versus Case Outcome**

| | | Case Outcome | |
|---|---|---|---|
| | | COIN Loss | COIN Win |
| Both "crush them" factors | Yes | 18 | 2 |
| | No | 4 | 6 |

***Repression in the Phases.*** At the case level, the employment of collective punishment and escalating repression proved to be quite detrimental, with the vast majority of losing COIN forces using both (18 of 22) and only two of eight COIN winners doing so. These findings partially reverse at the phase level. In 19 intermediate phases, the COIN force had the upper hand but went on to lose the case to the insurgents. In 17 of these 19 phases, both "crush them" factors were present. This shows that repression *can* win phases but is likely to lead to a loss in the long run. It appears that Abraham Lincoln was correct: "Force is all-conquering, but its victories are short-lived."

**Amnesty/Rewards.** This category represents less a full approach to COIN than a set of practical advice. The benefits accruing to amnesty or reward programs could support the elements of many other approaches. An amnesty program is usually one of the first steps toward establishing an effective disarmament, demobilization, and reintegration process.[37]

---

[37] For further reading on the disarmament, demobilization, and reintegration process, see Macartan Humphreys and Jeremy M. Weinstein, "Demobilization and Reintegration," *Journal of Conflict Resolution*, Vol. 51, No. 4, 2007; Jeremy Weinstein and Macartan Humphreys, *Disentangling the Determinants of Successful Demobilization and Reintegration*, Working Paper No. 69, Washington, D.C.: Center for Global Development, 2005; and Nicole Ball and Luc van de Goor, *Disarmament, Demobilization and Reintegration: Mapping Issues, Dilemmas and Guiding Principles*, Clingendael, Netherlands: Netherlands Institute of International Relations, August 2006.

The logic and tenets are simple:[38]

- Amnesty is a potentially attractive option for insurgents, reducing the need for a "fight to the finish."
- Even expensive rewards can be more cost-effective than large-scale military operations.

Two factors represent amnesty in this analysis:

- An amnesty or reward program was in place.
- The amnesty program reduced the number of insurgents.

The empirical cut point required both factors. All five cases that had an effective amnesty program in the decisive phase were wins for the COIN side. (See Table 3.13.) While this appears to offer strong support for this approach, two shortcomings in our analysis require that we temper our support. First, the effectiveness of an amnesty program hinges on a number of variables but mostly on the attractiveness of the offer relative to alternatives. The attractiveness of an amnesty offer depends in part on the insurgents' perceptions of their prospects for success. This leaves this factor as partially tautological: If you

**Table 3.13**
**Both Amnesty Factors Versus Case Outcome**

| | | Case Outcome | |
|---|---|---|---|
| | | COIN Loss | COIN Win |
| Both amnesty factors | Yes | 0 | 5 |
| | No | 22 | 3 |

[38] Long, 2006, pp. 45–49.

are beating the insurgents, they are more likely to accept your amnesty. Second is the issue of causal ordering. Does the COIN force win because it offers amnesty, or does the COIN force offer amnesty because it is winning? Our phases are not sufficiently fine-grained to discriminate the sequence of events enough to tell. If we are just interested in correlation, then it does not really matter: Effective amnesty programs co-occur with COIN wins. If we are interested in plausible causal explanations (as we are), then our analysis is not well structured to adjudicate the contribution of this approach. What we *can* tell from our data is that we do not reject this approach. That is, while we cannot determine whether winners offered amnesty or amnesty offers led to victory, we can tell that amnesty is correlated with victory: Amnesty does not lead to insurgent victory.

This is really an approach to easing and accelerating the end of an insurgency and less about actually defeating it. Our analysis is structured to discriminate victory from loss, not to consider the nuance of timing, the quality of the win or loss, or transitions from conflict to peace. *Because of the relationship of amnesty to our analysis, we cannot properly test it.*

### Contemporary Approaches to COIN

**Strategic Communication.** Strategic communication is a relatively recent term of art for coordinated whole-of-government persuasion and influence efforts. When applied to the COIN context, it suggests a population-centric and legitimacy-based approach for which we have distilled the following tenets:

- Maintain credibility.
- Minimize the "say-do" gap.
- Prioritize consistency of message.
- Continuity of message over time improves credibility.
- Kinetic and nonkinetic messaging is noncontradictory.
- Core messages flow from policy goals.
- There is unity of effort.
- Core themes contribute to COIN operational goals.
- There is expectation management.

Capturing the essence of strategic communication as an approach to COIN is challenging. None of the COIN literature predating the turn of the current century explicitly mentions strategic communication, simply because the term was not yet in use. Lacking a period synonym, much of relevance to strategic communication can be found in COIN discussions of psychological operations (PSYOP), information operations (IO), and propaganda or simply as subtext among the principles and theories of COIN.

Though no one explicitly articulates a theory of strategic communication for COIN, there are sufficiently clear statements and recommendations in the literature to extrapolate a strategic communication COIN approach.[39] Existing work on strategic communication implies that, done correctly, strategic communication can deliver the support (or at least tacit approval) of an indigenous population, reduce support for an insurgency, and sometimes influence the behavior of insurgents themselves. Strategic communication is *not* posited as a sufficient solution to the challenge of COIN—that is, no one suggests that effective strategic communication alone is enough to end an insurgency. Strategic communication is variously held to be a force multiplier or one important pillar in a multipronged approach to countering insurgency.

Strategic communication was represented in the analysis by seven factors:

- COIN force and government actions were consistent with messages (delivering on promises).
- The COIN force maintained credibility with populations in the area of conflict (includes expectation management).

---

[39] See, for example Mari K. Eder, "Toward Strategic Communication," *Military Review*, July–August 2007; Richard J. Josten, "Strategic Communication: Key Enabler for Elements of National Power," *IO Sphere*, Summer 2006; Jeffrey B. Jones, "Strategic Communication: A Mandate for the United States," *Joint Force Quarterly*, No. 39, 4th Quarter 2005; Richard Halloran, "Strategic Communication," *Parameters*, Autumn 2007; Christopher Paul, *Information Operations—Doctrine and Practice: A Handbook*, Westport, Conn.: Praeger Security International, 2008; and David P. Anders, *Developing an Operational Level Strategic Communication Model for Counterinsurgency*, Carlisle, Pa.: U.S. Army War College, 2009.

- Messages or themes cohered with the overall COIN approach.
- COIN forces avoided creating unattainable expectations.
- Themes and messages were coordinated across all involved government agencies.
- There was an earnest IO/PSYOP/strategic communication/messaging effort.
- Unity of effort or unity of command was maintained.

As noted elsewhere in this monograph, approaches to COIN are not mutually exclusive and often have tenets and, thus, factors in common. However, all seven of these factors are unique to strategic communication in this analysis. (That is, none of these factors also appears in another approach.)

The empirical cut point for the sum of strategic communication factors present in a given case was two or more, so we considered strategic communication to have been employed in any case in which at least two of these seven strategic communication factors were present.

*Strategic communication as an approach to COIN receives strong support in this analysis.* In all eight cases in which the COIN force prevailed, it employed at least two strategic communication factors; in only two cases in which the COIN force lost did it employ at least two strategic communication factors. (See Table 3.14.)

**Table 3.14**
**At Least Two Strategic Communication Factors Versus Case Outcome**

| | | Case Outcome | |
|---|---|---|---|
| | | COIN Loss | COIN Win |
| At least two strategic communication factors | Yes | 2 | 8 |
| | No | 20 | 0 |

Of the seven factors chosen to represent strategic communication, six of them each appear exactly five times in the eight cases won by the COIN force. This means that it is not always the same factor or pair of factors accounting for the "at least two" criterion and that the number of factors could not be significantly reduced without risking the loss of some of the approach's (considerable) predictive power.

**COIN FM.** FM 3-24, *Counterinsurgency*, is the U.S. Army and U.S. Marine Corps' collective attempt to update their doctrine to address the changes in COIN since the end of the Cold War.[40] The approach implicit in FM 3-24 has these tenets:

- Provide security.
- Establish government capabilities.
- Provide basic services.
- Address grievances.
- Reduce corruption.
- All of the above help separate the insurgents from the population, and attendant popular support improves intelligence collection and contributes to legitimacy.

FM 3-24 contains a population-centric approach to COIN with an emphasis on security, development, positive relations, and legitimacy. It is a hybrid built by combining traditional COIN approaches with new insights. According to FM 3-24, legitimacy is the main objective of COIN forces, and, as such, all operations should be undertaken with consideration for the effect they have on the legitimacy of the COIN force and the host-nation government.[41]

This approach is clearly a popular support–based theory, but it makes explicit connections between popular support and COIN enablers, such as improved intelligence, reduction of inputs needed by insurgents, and a relationship between support and COIN force

[40] See Headquarters, U.S. Department of the Army, and Headquarters, U.S. Marine Corps, 2007.

[41] Headquarters, U.S. Department of the Army, and Headquarters, U.S. Marine Corps, 2007, p. 38.

or government legitimacy—the ultimate goal of a COIN operation, according to this perspective.

Critics of FM 3-24 have attacked the document for some of its directives, suggesting that many of the principles set forth by the authors make soldiers and marines less safe and more vulnerable. Perhaps in an effort to respond to these naysayers, some of the U.S. military's brightest COIN theorists and practitioners weighed in with an article titled "Principles, Imperatives, and Paradoxes of Counterinsurgency." In this brief article, published in the March–April 2006 issue of *Military Review*, the authors set forth to defend the following COIN paradoxes extracted from FM 3-24:[42]

- The more you protect your force, the less secure you are.
- The more force you use, the less effective you are.
- Sometimes doing nothing is the best reaction.
- The best weapons for COIN do not fire bullets.
- Indigenous forces doing something poorly is sometimes better than COIN forces doing it well.
- If a tactic works this week, it will not work next week; if it works in this province, it will not work in the next.
- Tactical success is not a guarantee of COIN campaign success.

FM 3-24 was represented in our analysis by nine factors:

- A perception of security was created or maintained among populations in areas that the COIN force claimed to control.
- Government corruption was reduced or good governance increased since the onset of the conflict.
- Insurgent-claimed grievances were substantially addressed since the onset of the conflict
- The COIN force sought to engage and establish positive relations with the population in the area of conflict.
- The COIN force provided or ensured the provision of basic services in areas that it controlled or claimed to control.

---

[42] Cohen et al., 2006.

- There were short-term investments, improvements in infrastructure or development, or property reform in the area controlled or claimed by the COIN force.
- COIN forces received substantial intelligence from a population in the area of conflict.
- The majority of the population in the area of conflict supported or favored the COIN force.
- The COIN force avoided culturally offensive behaviors and messages.

As a blend of classic and contemporary COIN thinking, the approach implicit in FM 3-24 shares several of these factors with other COIN approaches. The empirical cut point for the summation of these nine factors was three, so the factor stack representing FM 3-24 is "at least three COIN FM factors present."

*FM 3-24 receives strong empirical support*, with seven of eight COIN wins having at least three COIN FM factors and only one COIN loss having three or more of these factors. (The one win without was Croatia; the loss with was Kampuchea.) That leaves the approach one win and one loss away from perfectly explaining the data all by itself. (See Table 3.15.)

Of the specific factors, three are noteworthy in that they appear only in cases in which the COIN force won: "Government corruption

**Table 3.15**
**At Least Three COIN FM Factors Versus Case Outcome**

| At least three COIN FM factors | | Case Outcome: COIN Loss | Case Outcome: COIN Win |
|---|---|---|---|
| | Yes | 1 | 8 |
| | No | 21 | 0 |

reduced/good governance increased since onset of conflict" was present in three wins (no losses), "COIN force sought to engage and establish positive relations with population in area of conflict" was present in four wins (no losses), and "Short-term investments, improvements in infrastructure/development, or property reform in area of conflict controlled or claimed by COIN force" was present in five wins (no losses).

**"Beat Cop."** The beat-cop approach is concerned with the employment of the COIN force. If the COIN force is routinely present in the communities in the area of conflict and conducts regular dismount patrols—becoming individually familiar with and known to the local population (in the manner of the traditional urban beat cop)—then numerous advantages are envisioned to accrue to the COIN force. Such community policing or regular dismount patrolling in the mode of a beat cop

- enables intelligence collection
- creates greater understanding of the local situation
- deters criminal activity
- deters insurgent support and activity
- creates trust between the COIN force and the population.[43]

Various beat-cop approaches imply a subordinate form of the more general pacification approach and are closely aligned with population-centric COIN theory. The beat-cop approach is implicit in much of the advice offered in FM 3-24, which places the onus on soldiers and marines to connect with the population they seek to protect. At its core, this approach is about establishing and maintaining trust with the locals. As David Kilcullen asserts, "For your side to win, the people do not have to like you but they must respect you, accept that your actions benefit them, and trust your integrity and ability to deliver on promises, particularly regarding their security."[44]

---

[43] Headquarters, U.S. Department of the Army, and Headquarters, U.S. Marine Corps, 2007, pp. 229–231.

[44] Kilcullen, 2006a, p. 29.

Familiarity breeds trust, which, in turn, can lead the COIN force to garner intelligence. While fundamentally in agreement with the core principles of pacification approaches, these practices are focused on how best to employ security forces in a pacified or partially pacified area.

The beat-cop corollary to pacification approaches is represented in our analysis by six factors:

- The perception of security was created or maintained among populations in areas that the COIN force claimed to control.
- The COIN force employed local militias or irregular forces or engaged in or enabled community policing in areas that it controlled or claimed to control.
- Militias did not work at cross-purposes with COIN or government forces.
- The COIN force received substantial intelligence from a population in the area of conflict.
- In the area of conflict, the COIN force was *not* perceived as worse than the insurgents.
- The COIN force sought to engage and establish positive relations with the population in the area of conflict.

The empirical cut point for the beat-cop approach was at least two of these six factors. Twelve cases had at least two factors present. Of those, eight were COIN wins and four were COIN losses. (See Table 3.16.) Based on this evidence, *the beat-cop approach receives strong support.*

***A Word About Militias.*** Several approaches (including beat cop) call for the use of local militias to extend armed presence or allow locals to have a stake in their own security.[45] Recent successes in Iraq have

[45] Historical examples of militias used in COIN operations include the Popular Forces, the Civilian Irregular Defense Groups, and the People's Self-Defense Forces in Vietnam and the *quadrillage* in Algeria, although, as Austin Long points out, the forces used by the *quadrillage* were mainly regular troops instead of locals (Long, 2006, p. 54).

**Table 3.16**
**At Least Two "Beat-Cop" Factors Versus Case Outcome**

| At least two "beat-cop" factors | Case Outcome: COIN Loss | Case Outcome: COIN Win |
|---|---|---|
| Yes | 4 | 8 |
| No | 18 | 0 |

made militias more prominent in contemporary discussions.[46] This research provides mixed evidence on militias. During development of the case studies, we quickly realized that the creation or fostering of militias could lead to both positive and negative results. Indeed, we inductively added a factor, "Militias did *not* work at cross-purposes with COIN force/government," which we also added as a factor to any approach that recommends militias. Fully 25 of our cases employed militias or otherwise enabled community policing. Six of those 25 cases were COIN wins, and 19 were losses. The use of militias alone is unrelated to outcome. When militias that worked at cross-purposes with the COIN force or the government are removed, however, a modest relationship between militias and COIN success appears: Four cases in which the COIN force won employed militias that did not work at cross-purposes with the government, as did six COIN losses.

A word of caution: None of the COIN forces that armed and recruited militias *wanted* them to work at cross-purposes, but more than half (15 of 25) *did*, and with disastrous results (13 of 15 cases in which a militia worked at cross-purposes with the government were COIN losses). This supports a recommendation for extreme caution in the use of militias in support of COIN.

---

[46] See Austin Long, "The Anbar Awakening," *Survival*, Vol. 50, No. 2, April–May 2008.

**"Boots on the Ground."** Without articulating exactly why, several scholars and observers insist on a certain minimum force ratio either between counterinsurgents and insurgents or between COIN forces and the population. See for example, James Quinlivan's foundational research in this area, which reports historical ratios of security forces to population for a number of stability operations;[47] FM 3-24, which advocates a troop density of approximately 20–25 counterinsurgents per 1,000 residents;[48] and Douglas Ollivant and Eric Chewning, who advocate a 10-to-1 or 20-to-1 ratio of counterinsurgents to insurgents to prevent the development of insurgent safe areas.[49] The logic behind "boots on the ground" would presumably follow pacification approaches, though it might also include elements of legitimacy associated with force presence or connect to traditional military theory concerned with the minimum sufficient force with which to conduct certain types of operations. Indeed, we can see elements of this debate playing out in the political sphere as various individuals and groups advocate for or against a proposed "surge" of troops in Afghanistan similar to that which took effect in Iraq in 2007. As far as we can discern, those advocating "boots on the ground" see the following advantages:

- The presence of forces deters adversary action and reassures the population.
- COIN requires a certain amount of infantry presence spread throughout the contested area.[50]

These are testable tenets and so are sufficient for this analysis. This approach to COIN is represented by four factors in our analysis:

---

[47] James T. Quinlivan, "Force Requirements in Stability Operations," *Parameters*, Winter 1995.

[48] Headquarters, U.S. Department of the Army, and Headquarters, U.S. Marine Corps, 2007, p. 23.

[49] Douglas A. Ollivant and Eric D. Chewning, "Producing Victory: Rethinking Conventional Forces in COIN Operations," *Military Review*, July–August 2006, p. 52.

[50] Ollivant and Chewning, 2006, p. 52.

- The perception of security was created or maintained among populations in areas that the COIN force claimed to control.
- The COIN force employed local militias or irregular forces or engaged in or enabled community policing in areas that it controlled or claimed to control.
- The COIN force sought to engage and establish positive relations with the population in the area of conflict.
- *No* parts of the area of conflict were no-go or otherwise denied to the COIN force.

The summation of "boots on the ground" factors versus case outcome shows that at least two of the four factors is the empirical cut point. Six of the eight cases in which the COIN force won had at least two boots on the ground factors, while only two COIN losses did. (See Table 3.17.) *This constitutes evidence in strong support of the boots on the ground approach.*

Note that this factor stack includes the use of militias and does not actively exclude militias that worked at cross-purposes. Apparently, using militias and realizing one or more of the other boots on the ground factors correlates with militias not working at cross-purposes or diminishes the negative effects of such behavior.

**Table 3.17**
**At Least Two "Boots on the Ground" Factors Versus Case Outcome**

| At least two "boots on the ground" factors | | Case Outcome: COIN Loss | Case Outcome: COIN Win |
|---|---|---|---|
| | Yes | 2 | 6 |
| | No | 20 | 2 |

**"Put a Local Face on It."** A piece of practical advice from contemporary operations advises the COIN force to seek to "put a local face on it."[51] This advice implies that local communities in insurgent-contested areas do need security and development following the logic of generic pacification approaches, and their provision through well-prepared indigenous forces has several advantages and avoids several possible pitfalls of having foreign forces serve in that role. Tenets include the following:

- Invest in training, developing, and equipping local security forces.[52]
- Indigenous forces may need training in the use of measured force, in addition to other COIN training.[53]
- Appropriate indigenous actors will know the culture and will be less vexing to the population (if they restrain themselves to proportional force).[54]
- Indigenous forces can form (or may already have) long-term relationships that facilitate the COIN effort.[55]
- Indigenous forces need to develop sustainable security capabilities before foreign COIN forces can leave.[56]

This approach harkens back to the time of classic counterinsurgent and well-known Arabist T. E. Lawrence, who famously quipped, "Better the Arabs do it tolerably than you do it perfectly."[57]

---

[51] David H. Petraeus, "Learning Counterinsurgency: Observations from Soldiering in Iraq," *Military Review*, January–February 2006, pp. 3–4.

[52] Headquarters, U.S. Department of the Army, and Headquarters, U.S. Marine Corps, 2007, pp. 199–235.

[53] Sepp, 2005, p. 11.

[54] Gompert et al., 2008, p. 81. See also Headquarters, U.S. Department of the Army, and Headquarters, U.S. Marine Corps, 2007, p. 247.

[55] James S. Corum, *Training Indigenous Forces in Counterinsurgency: A Tale of Two Insurgencies*, Carlisle, Pa.: Strategic Studies Institute, U.S. Army War College, March 2006.

[56] Sepp, 2005, p. 12.

[57] T. E. Lawrence, "The Twenty-Seven Articles," *The Arab Bulletin*, August 20, 1917.

The greatest difficulty here is finding indigenous forces that are up to the task of conducting COIN operations that meet U.S. standards. Even after months and years of training, some indigenous forces still may not be able to reach a level acceptable to U.S. military trainers. This poses an obvious dilemma related to timetables for withdrawal and the consequences of being perceived as occupiers.

Like all pacification-related approaches, this is a population-centric approach to COIN. This COIN advice is predicated on the assumption that the primary COIN force is from out of town—either an extranational force (as the United States will always be as a COIN actor) or a national force that is sufficiently culturally different to be considered "foreign" by the locals.[58]

Four factors represent this corollary approach in our analysis:

- The COIN force employed local militias or irregular forces or engaged in or enabled community policing in areas that it controlled or claimed to control.
- The COIN force did *not* employ culturally inappropriate outsiders for a significant fraction of operations.
- Indigenous forces conducted the majority of COIN operations.
- Militias did *not* work at cross-purposes with COIN or government forces.

Many COIN forces did one or more of these things in multiple cases, both wins and losses. While normally that would be strong evidence against an approach (it does not matter for the outcome whether these things were done or not), this approach is not meant to apply to all cases. "Put a local face on it" is advice only to forces conducting COIN outside their native country. The primary COIN force was from another country in only three of the 30 cases in this analysis, and none of them did any of these things. Without any variation in the data for the subset of cases for which this approach is relevant, *we cannot test "put a local face on it" with these data.*

---

[58] An example of the latter point is Russian COIN forces fighting in Chechnya.

**Cultural Awareness.** Offered as necessary but certainly not sufficient is the proposition that cultural awareness is critical to COIN success. The tenets are straightforward and have clear validity:

- Cultural insensitivity can undermine otherwise successful COIN practices.
- Good cultural awareness is an enabler.
- Without understanding of culture, much intelligence cannot be understood and will likely be improperly applied.[59]

This supporting approach is relevant only when the COIN force (by virtue of being composed of outsiders or culturally dissimilar indigenes) is not culturally "native" to the area of conflict. In the modern era of instant communication, a seemingly innocent cultural faux pas can be disseminated around the globe in minutes, exposing the COIN force to worldwide criticism and portraying a negative image for all to see.

Furthermore, just as with the United States in Japan following World War II, unfamiliarity with language and culture forces an occupier or COIN force to rely more on the locals and any preexisting political, bureaucratic, and social structures.[60]

This corollary to other COIN approaches is intended to apply only where the COIN force is not culturally similar to the population in the area of conflict. It is represented by three factors in our analysis:

- The COIN force did *not* employ culturally inappropriate outsiders for a significant fraction of operations.
- The COIN force avoided culturally offensive behaviors and messages.
- COIN or government actions did not contribute to substantial new grievances claimed by the insurgents.

---

[59] Headquarters, U.S. Department of the Army, and Headquarters, U.S. Marine Corps, 2007, p. 41.

[60] David Edelstein, "Occupational Hazards: Why Military Occupations Succeed or Fail," *International Security*, Vol. 29, No. 1, Summer 2004, p. 67.

Twenty-nine of the 30 cases had at least one of these factors in the decisive phase. This is no doubt because in 27 of the 30 cases, indigenous forces were the primary COIN actors, and cultural difference was not expected to be present or consequential. Because of the small number of cases to which this corollary would apply, *we cannot test cultural awareness in this analysis.*

**Tangible Support Reduction.** What we call the "tangible support reduction approach" is a contemporary spin on cost-benefit and popular support–based approaches. This perspective follows the cost-benefit approach in suggesting that it is the support the insurgents receive, from wherever they get it, that is the real center of gravity.[61] Tenets include the following:[62]

- Insurgencies need manpower, funding, materiel, sanctuary, intelligence,[63] and tolerance.[64]
- These needs can be met through self-supply, looting, purchasing, or reliance on an external source.[65]
- External sources could be local populations, state sponsors, diaspora communities, or other groups within or outside the area of conflict.
- Effective COIN interrupts the supply of support to insurgents.

This approach does not take the full "systems" approach of the classic cost-benefit approach but simply suggests that the COIN force

---

[61] Christopher Paul, "How Do Terrorists Generate and Maintain Support?" in Paul K. Davis and Kim Cragin, eds., *Social Science for Counterterrorism: Putting the Pieces Together*, Santa Monica, Calif.: RAND Corporation, MG-849-OSD, 2009.

[62] Christopher Paul, "As a Fish Swims in the Sea: Relationships Between Factors Contributing to Support for Terrorist or Insurgent Groups," *Studies in Conflict and Terrorism*, Vol. 33, No. 6, 2010.

[63] Steven Metz and Raymond Millen, *Insurgency and Counterinsurgency in the 21st Century: Reconceptualizing Threat and Response*, Carlisle, Pa.: Strategic Studies Institute, U.S. Army War College, November 2004.

[64] Paul, 2009.

[65] Anthony Vinci, "The 'Problems of Mobilization' and the Analysis of Armed Groups," *Parameters*, Spring 2006, p. 51.

identify and focus on depriving the insurgents of the sources of support on which they actually rely. When the insurgents draw significant support from the population, this approach is wholly consonant with popular support–based approaches.

Insurgents' many support needs can be met in myriad ways. Ten factors were indentified to represent this from a COIN perspective in our analysis:

- The flow of cross-border insurgent support significantly decreased or remained dramatically reduced or largely absent.
- Important external support to insurgents was significantly reduced.
- Important internal support to insurgents was significantly reduced.
- Insurgents' ability to replenish resources was significantly diminished.
- Insurgents were unable to maintain or grow their force size.
- COIN force efforts resulted in increased costs for insurgent processes.
- COIN forces effectively disrupted insurgent recruiting.
- COIN forces effectively disrupted insurgent materiel acquisition.
- COIN forces effectively disrupted insurgent intelligence.
- COIN forces effectively disrupted insurgent financing.

The empirical cut point for this set of factors proved to be three or more. All cases in which three or more tangible support reduction factors appeared were won by the COIN side. All eight COIN wins had at least three tangible support reduction factors, and no losses had more than two. This is the only factor stack in the analysis that perfectly predicts case outcomes. (See Table 3.18.) *This is extremely strong evidence in support of a tangible support reduction approach to COIN.*

***Tangible Support Versus Popular Support.*** Many of the approaches described and tested here are based on a population-centric theory of COIN. They maintain that the population is the center of gravity and that wooing the population, through legitimacy, security, investmentand services, or some combination of these or other things, will lead the population to renounce the insurgents, inform on them, vote against them, and *deny them materiel support.*

**Table 3.18**
**At Least Three Tangible Support Reduction Factors Versus Case Outcome**

| At least three tangible support reduction factors | Case Outcome: COIN Loss | Case Outcome: COIN Win |
|---|---|---|
| Yes | 0 | 8 |
| No | 22 | 0 |

If insurgents are meeting their support needs from the population in the area of conflict, then tangible support and popular support would be largely the same thing, and persuading that population to stop meeting the needs of the insurgents would be an effective tangible support reduction strategy. Are they the same, however?

In 25 of the 30 cases considered here, popular support and tangible support covaried. That is, when the insurgents had the support of the population, they were able to maintain their tangible support, and vice versa. The five cases in which these conditions did not correspond are quite instructional: In three cases, the COIN force had the support of the population but did not accrue at least three tangible support reduction factors. In all three of these cases, the insurgents prevailed. In two cases, the COIN force reduced at least three tangible insurgent support factors but did not gain the support of the population, yet the COIN force still won both.

This suggests an important caveat to the conventional wisdom that the population is *the* center of gravity. It appears that, in fact, *tangible support* is "the" center of gravity.[66] Tangible support usually

[66] *The* is in quotation marks here as a reminder that we reject a single-factor or unitary explanation of successful COIN that hinges on only one center of gravity. The whole argument that "victory has a thousand fathers" recognizes that a substantial collection of effective practices or a host of complementary lines of operation is what wins the day in COIN. To

(but not always) stems from or connects to popular support. When it does, treating the population as the center of gravity will lead to the desired outcome; that outcome is less certain when insurgents' tangible support does not come from the population. This supports advice presented elsewhere by the lead author that COIN forces should identify the specific support needs and sources of that support for their specific adversary.[67]

**Criticality of Intelligence.** Current COIN doctrine also asserts the criticality of actionable intelligence to COIN success.[68] Intelligence is clearly important to many of the approaches listed here. It is difficult to articulate specific tenets without making explicit the individual connections to some of the broader approaches. Generally, statements on this approach offer a single tenet:

- Actionable intelligence drives successful COIN operations.

This approach is captured in the analysis by two factors:

- Intelligence was adequate to support kill/capture or engagements on the COIN force's terms.
- Intelligence was adequate to allow COIN forces to disrupt insurgent processes or operations.

The empirical cut point is at least one of the two. Six of the eight cases won by COIN forces included at least one of these two intelligence factors, while both factors were absent in the losing cases.[69] (See Table 3.19.) This is *strong evidence in support of the criticality of intelligence.*

---

the extent that one area of COIN emphasis is primary, however, these analyses suggest that tangible support is more critical than popular support and that the distinction is immaterial when insurgent tangible support needs are met primarily by the population.

[67] Paul, 2010.

[68] Headquarters, U.S. Department of the Army, and Headquarters, U.S. Marine Corps, 2007, p. 41.

[69] The two cases in which the COIN force managed to prevail without at least one intelligence factor present were El Salvador and Uganda.

**Table 3.19**
**At Least One Intelligence Factor Versus Case Outcome**

| | | Case Outcome: COIN Loss | Case Outcome: COIN Win |
|---|---|---|---|
| At least one intelligence factor | Yes | 0 | 6 |
| | No | 22 | 2 |

Of the two individual factors, all of the predictive power adheres to "Intelligence adequate to allow COIN force to disrupt insurgent processes or operations," as it appears in all six of the COIN wins containing either factor. "Intelligence adequate to support kill/capture or engagements on COIN force's terms" appears only jointly with "Intelligence adequate to allow COIN force to disrupt insurgent processes or operations."

**Flexibility and Adaptability.** Overwhelming firepower and sophisticated technology have never been a guarantors of victory in COIN operations. At no time has this been truer than in today's operating environment, where insurgents use the Internet to great effect and use rudimentary materials to construct increasingly deadly improvised explosive devices to counter COIN forces. John Nagl's *Learning to Eat Soup with a Knife* emphasizes the importance of the COIN force's ability to adapt quickly and effectively to changes in warfare.[70] This practical advice (flexibility and adaptability) extends to other, broader approaches to COIN. The tenets are simple:

70 Nagl, 2005.

- COIN is a two-player game against an adaptive adversary.
- A successful COIN force must learn and adapt.[71]

The insistence that only an adaptive COIN force can prevail is represented by a single factor:

- The COIN force did *not* fail to adapt to changes in adversary strategy, operations, or tactics.

All eight COIN forces that prevailed avoided failure to adapt, as did six of the losing COIN forces. (See Table 3.20.) This constitutes *strong evidence in support of the importance of flexibility and adaptability.*

We score this factor as strongly supported, even though six COIN forces that were adaptable failed, because this approach does not purport to be sufficient, only necessary, and it satisfies the minimum preconditions for necessity: No case was won by a force that failed to adapt. In fact, no phase was won by a COIN force that failed to adapt. (See the section "Phase Outcomes" in Chapter Four.)

The case-level analysis showed that in no case in which the COIN force failed to adapt did it prevail. This holds at the phase level as well.

**Table 3.20**
**Flexibility and Adaptability Versus Case Outcome**

| | | Case Outcome | |
|---|---|---|---|
| | | COIN Loss | COIN Win |
| Flexibility and adaptability | Yes | 6 | 8 |
| | No | 16 | 0 |

[71] Headquarters, U.S. Department of the Army, and Headquarters, U.S. Marine Corps, 2007, p. 46.

In no phase in which the COIN force failed to adapt did it end the phase with the upper hand. However, it remains possible for the inflexible to recover. In four cases, the COIN force failed to adapt (and did not have the upper hand) in an intermediate phase but ultimately prevailed in the case.

### Insurgent Approaches

COIN forces are not the only side writing on strategic and theoretical matters. While not the primary interest of this monograph, insurgents have a long-established history of strategic thought and writing as well, with classic texts authored by Mao Tse-Tung (*On Guerrilla Warfare*), Ernesto "Che" Guevara (*Guerrilla Warfare*), and the Provisional Irish Republican Army's widely disseminated training manual known as the "Green Book."[72] The Internet has contributed to a proliferation of such writings, especially by such groups as al Qaeda and others, which have written extensively on issues ranging from best practices in insurgent warfare to rules of war against adversaries.[73]

As explained in detail in FM 3-24, counterinsurgents have a difficult task in attempting to discern not only the insurgents' motivation but also the approach being used to wage the insurgency. While history provides a plethora of approaches used by insurgents, some of the more contemporarily relevant ones are discussed here:[74]

- *Protracted popular war:* Advocated by Mao, protracted popular war outlines a three-phased approach involving both military and political elements, including strategic defense, strategic stalemate,

---

[72] Other classic insurgent works include Vo Nguyen Giap's *People's War People's Army: The Vietcong Insurrection Manual for Underdeveloped Countries*, Regis Debray's *Revolution in the Revolution,* Carlos Marighella's *Minimanual of the Urban Guerrilla*, and Abraham Guillen's *Philosophy of the Urban Guerrilla.*

[73] Two such writings include Ayman al-Zawahiri's *Knights under the Prophet's Banner* and Mustafa Setmariam Nasar's (a.k.a. Abu Musab al-Suri) *The Global Islamic Resistance Call.*

[74] Other insurgent approaches not discussed in detail here are conspiratorial (Marxist-Leninist), identity-focused, composite, and coalition.

and strategic counteroffense.[75] This approach was used by insurgents in both Peru and Nepal.

- *Military-focused:* Popularized by Che Guevara and also referred to as the "focoist approach," this strategy entails a small group of guerrillas operating in a rural environment where the grievances of the local population can be easily exploited to build the conditions necessary to overthrow a government.[76] This approach was used by the Sandinistas in Nicaragua.
- *Urban:* The urban approach, pursued most ardently by the Provisional Irish Republican Army, includes sowing disorder by inciting sectarian violence, weakening the government, intimidating the population, targeting government and opposition leaders, intimidating police and military forces, and provoking government repression.[77]

**Insurgent Support Strategies.** FM 3-24 points out several elements or tenets of insurgent-side approaches:[78]

- demonstration of potency through attack
- coercion (a cost-benefit strategy)
- encouraging COIN force overreaction
- use of apolitical fighters
- development of counterinstitutions (related to legitimacy).

---

[75] For a more in-depth treatment of Mao's theory of protracted war, see Headquarters, U.S. Department of the Army, and Headquarters, U.S. Marine Corps, 2007, pp. 11–13. For more information on Maoism in general, including Mao's "Six Main Points for Attention" and emphasis on the political element of waging an insurgency, see Thomas X. Hammes, *The Sling and the Stone: On War in the 21st Century*, St. Paul, Minn.: Zenith Press, 2004, pp. 44–55. Reprints of Mao's original works include *On Protracted War*, Peking: People's Publishing House, 1954, and *Guerrilla Warfare.*

[76] For a cogent discussion of the focoist approach to insurgency, see Hammes, 2004, p. 77.

[77] Headquarters, U.S. Department of the Army, and Headquarters, U.S. Marine Corps, 2007, p. 10.

[78] Headquarters, U.S. Department of the Army, and Headquarters, U.S. Marine Corps, 2007, p. 105.

The various insurgent support strategies are represented in the analysis by three factors:

- The insurgents demonstrated potency through attacks.
- The insurgents discredited or delegitimized the COIN force or the government.
- The insurgents provided or ensured the provision of basic services in areas that they controlled or claimed to control.

There is no empirical cut point for the sum of these factors, and they distribute fairly evenly across both wins and losses. (See Table 3.21.) At least one of these three factors is present in all but one case; requiring two or three of these factors still gives a fairly even distribution between wins and losses. Thus, there is a minimal correlation between insurgent support strategies and case outcomes. This lack of association is *strong evidence against the importance of these insurgent support strategies.*

**Table 3.21**
**Number of Insurgent Support Strategy Factors Versus Case Outcome**

| | | Case Outcome | |
|---|---|---|---|
| | | COIN Loss | COIN Win |
| Number of insurgent support strategy factors | 3 | 4 | 1 |
| | 2 | 15 | 4 |
| | 1 | 3 | 2 |
| | 0 | 0 | 1 |

**Continuation and Contestation.** In the same vein, several scholars suggest that insurgents win simply by not losing.[79] Steven Metz and Raymond Millen articulate this approach explicitly as continuation and contestation, with the following tenets.[80]

[79] Cohen et al., 2006, p. 51.

[80] Metz and Millen, 2004, p. 6.

- The insurgents maintain force protection.
- The insurgents delegitimize the COIN or the government.
- The insurgents maintain an open supply of resources.

This view is represented by four factors:

- The insurgents maintained or grew their force size.
- The insurgents discredited or delegitimized the COIN force or the government.
- The insurgents' ability to replenish resources was *not* significantly diminished.
- The insurgents avoided critical strategic errors or failure to make obvious adaptations, or they voluntarily exited the conflict.

The empirical cut point for this factor stack is all four factors. In all cases in which all four continuation and contestation factors were present in the decisive phase, the COIN force lost. That occurred in 18 of the 22 COIN losses and (obviously) no COIN wins. (See Table 3.22.) This strong predictive relationship is *strong evidence in support of continuation and contestation*. If insurgents can hang on until the end, they appear to prevail. The robustness of this finding would be dramatically increased with a complementary analysis of the

**Table 3.22**
**All Four Continuation and Contestation Factors Versus Case Outcome**

| All four continuation and contestation factors | | Case Outcome: COIN Loss | Case Outcome: COIN Win |
|---|---|---|---|
| | Yes | 18 | 0 |
| | No | 4 | 8 |

duration of insurgencies (i.e., What determines when an insurgency is in its decisive or terminal phase?), but that is beyond the scope of this analysis.

## Summary of the Tests of the Approaches

The matrix at the end of this volume lists all the factors that compose the factor stacks for the 20 COIN approaches tested in this chapter (there are a total of 57 factors). The row headers in the matrix correspond to the 20 approaches, and the column footers list the specific factors that represent these approaches; the colored cells match the factors with the approaches they represent.

In addition to being a useful summary, the matrix also shows where factors are included in multiple approaches (remember that these approaches to COIN are not mutually exclusive). When a factor has many colored cells in its column, that is indicative of its inclusion in many approaches. See, for example, the factor "Perception of security created or maintained among population in areas COIN force claimed to control," which is common to five different approaches, and "COIN force sought to engage and establish positive relations with population in area of conflict," which is common to three.

Table 3.23 summarizes the results for each approach. Each approach is listed, along with whether it received strong support from the evidence in our analysis, received some support from the evidence, received strong evidence against, or could not be tested. As reported at the beginning of this chapter, we assessed strength of support based on the approach's ability (by way of its factor stack) to predict or discriminate between case outcomes. Approaches were considered to have strong support if the bivariate relationship between the approach's factor stack and the outcome was very strong (i.e., using it and it alone is a very strong indicator of the outcome); some support if there was a moderately strong correlation between the approach's factor stack and the outcome but the approach's application occurred in a significant number of COIN losses; strong evidence against if the approach's application

**Table 3.23**
**Strength of Evidentiary Support for 20 Approaches to COIN**

| Approach | Factor/Factor Stack | COIN Losses Implementing Approach (of 22) | COIN Wins Implementing Approach (of 8) | Degree of Evidentiary Support |
|---|---|---|---|---|
| **Development** | **Both development factors** | **0** | **4** | **Strong support** |
| **Pacification** | **At least one of three pacification factors** | **1** | **8** | **Strong support** |
| **Legitimacy (government)** | **At least two of five government legitimacy factors** | **3** | **7** | **Strong support** |
| Legitimacy (use of force) | At least three of five legitimate use of force factors | 4 | 6 | Some support |
| Democracy | At least one of three democracy factors | 7 | 8 | Some support |
| Resettlement | Resettlement employed | 8 | 1 | Strong evidence against |
| **Cost-benefit** | **At least two of six cost-benefit factors** | **2** | **8** | **Strong support** |
| **Border control** | **Flow of cross-border insurgent support decreased or absent** | **1** | **8** | **Strong support** |
| "Crush them" | Both "crush them" factors | 18 | 2 | Strong evidence against |
| Amnesty/rewards | Both amnesty factors | 0 | 5 | Cannot be tested |
| **Strategic communication** | **At least two of seven strategic communication factors** | **2** | **8** | **Strong support** |
| **COIN FM** | **At least three of nine COIN FM factors** | **1** | **7** | **Strong support** |
| **"Beat cop"** | **At least two of six "beat-cop" factors** | **4** | **8** | **Strong support** |
| **"Boots on the ground"** | **At least two of four "boots on the ground" factors** | **2** | **6** | **Strong support** |

**Table 3.23—Continued**

| Approach | Factor/Factor Stack | COIN Losses Implementing Approach (of 22) | COIN Wins Implementing Approach (of 8) | Degree of Evidentiary Support |
|---|---|---|---|---|
| "Put a local face on it" | "Put a local face on it" | NA | NA | Cannot be tested |
| Cultural awareness | Cultural awareness | NA | NA | Cannot be tested |
| **Tangible support reduction** | **At least three of 10 tangible insurgent support factors reduced** | **0** | **8** | **Strong support** |
| **Criticality of intelligence** | **At least one of two intelligence factors** | **0** | **6** | **Strong support** |
| **Flexibility and adaptability** | **Flexibility and adaptability** | **6** | **8** | **Strong support** |
| Insurgent support strategies | At least one of three insurgent support factors | 22 | 7 | Strong evidence against |
| **Continuation and contestation** | **All four continuation and contestation factors** | **18** | **0** | **Strong support** |

predicted a greater proportion of losses than wins; and untestable if the approach was never applied.

As Table 3.23 shows, most of the approaches we tested receive at least some evidentiary support, with many (13) receiving strong support. For those approaches, this is a firm validation of advice drawn from common sense or based on a small number of cases. For those receiving strong evidence against—well, it is nice to be able to discriminate between those who have correctly identified the lessons of common sense or of small numbers of cases and those who have failed to do so.

The next chapter presents the results from our analyses and findings beyond the tests of these 20 distinct approaches to COIN.

CHAPTER FOUR

# Broader Findings

Chapter Three described and presented our tests of 20 approaches to COIN. This chapter describes and presents the results from analyses that consider *patterns of relationships* between multiple factors and the outcomes of the cases. Three analyses are presented. First, with so many of the approaches identified in the previous chapter receiving strong support, we try to preliminarily identify which patterns of factors occur most often in COIN wins. Our findings show that "good COIN practices run in packs" and that the balance of good versus bad COIN practices perfectly predicts the outcome in every case. From there, we then try to tease out which of the host of good COIN practices in the "pack" is most essential to success. Using a method called qualitative comparative analysis, we ask which of the 13 successful approaches to COIN supported by the evidence in the last chapter is the most causally central. This analysis, though ideally suited to that inquiry, finds that numerous patterns of supported approaches are equally central contributors to COIN success. This further validates the finding that good COIN practices run in packs and elevates its importance. Finally, we consider the broader patterns of outcomes in the intermediate phases of the 30 cases, finding that poor beginnings do not necessarily lead to poor outcomes. Each of these analyses is discussed in turn.

## Scorecard: Balance of Good Versus Bad Practices

In addition to the 57 factors (listed in the matrix at the end of this volume) that we selected to represent each approach and evaluated for each phase of each case, we identified 19 factors to evaluate for each phase of each case. We kept these 19 factors in the analysis as control variables. They were chosen based on other factors identified as important in the theoretical literature, our previous experience with research on correlates of urban instability,[1] and our preliminary readings of some of the historical cases. The additional factors are listed in the section "Factor Generation, Evaluation, and Scoring" in Appendix A. Further discussion of their selection and refinement can be found in the same section.

Preliminary analyses of the relationship of each factor with case outcomes, coupled with the analyses examining the factor stacks used to test the various approaches to COIN (presented in the previous chapter), revealed an interesting trend: Most approaches and factors that common sense dictated would have a positive relationship with COIN victories did; most factors that common sense suggested would lead to poor COIN outcomes by and large did so.

The persistent presence among COIN wins of so many factors representing different plausibly good approaches to COIN made it difficult to establish any priority or primacy among the various factors (as discussed later in this chapter). However, looking carefully at the patterns of factors present and absent in each case did reveal something very interesting: Every case won by the COIN force featured many factors that are part of demonstrably positive COIN practices or approaches and predominantly did not include detractive COIN factors; in instances in which the COIN force lost, this was never the case.

To confirm this preliminary observation, we gathered individual factors and factor stacks that had strong a priori grounding as good or bad COIN practices or that had strong bivariate relationships, whether

---

[1] Christopher Paul, Russell W. Glenn, Beth Grill, Megan P. McKernan, Barbara Raymond, Matt Stafford, and Horacio R. Trujillo, "Identifying Urban Flashpoints: A Delphi Derived Model for Scoring Cities' Vulnerability to Large-Scale Unrest," *Studies in Conflict and Terrorism*, Vol. 31, No. 11, 2008.

positive or negative, with the case outcome. We then took these factors or factor stacks and compiled them into 15 good COIN practices and 12 bad COIN practices (the "dirty dozen").

The good COIN practices or factors are as follows:

- The COIN force realized at least two strategic communication factors.
- The COIN force reduced at least three tangible insurgent support factors.
- The government realized at least two government legitimacy factors.
- The government realized at least one democracy factor.
- The COIN force realized at least one intelligence factor.
- The COIN force was of sufficient strength to force the insurgents to fight as guerrillas.
- The government or state was competent.
- The COIN force avoided excessive collateral damage, disproportionate use of force, or other illegitimate applications of force.
- The COIN force sought to engage and establish positive relations with the population in the area of conflict.
- Short-term investments, improvements in infrastructure or development, or property reform occurred in the area of conflict controlled or claimed by the COIN force.
- The majority of the population in the area of conflict supported or favored the COIN force.
- The COIN force established and then expanded secure areas.
- The COIN force had and used uncontested air dominance.
- The COIN force provided or ensured the provision of basic services in areas that it controlled or claimed to control.
- The perception of security was created or maintained among populations in areas that the COIN force claimed to control.

The bad COIN practices or factors are as follows:

- The COIN force used both collective punishment and escalating repression.
- The primary COIN force was an external occupier.
- COIN force or government actions contributed to substantial new grievances claimed by the insurgents.
- Militias worked at cross-purposes with the COIN force or government.
- The COIN force resettled or removed civilian populations for population control.
- COIN force collateral damage was perceived by the population in the area of conflict as worse than the insurgents'.
- In the area of conflict, the COIN force was perceived as worse than the insurgents.
- The COIN force failed to adapt to changes in adversary strategy, operations, or tactics.
- The COIN force engaged in more coercion or intimidation than the insurgents.
- The insurgent force was individually superior to the COIN force by being either more professional or better motivated.
- The COIN force or its allies relied on looting for sustainment.
- The COIN force and government had different goals or levels of commitment.

Taking the balance of the sum of good factors minus the sum of bad factors for each case provides a striking result: All of the cases in which the COIN force won have a significantly positive balance of good practices versus bad, while for all cases in which the COIN force lost, the balance is zero or negative (see Table 4.1). What is especially revealing is that the score for the highest-scoring loss is zero, while the score for the lowest-scoring win is five. This is a massive empirical separation—a gap that exposes wins and losses as fundamentally differentiated by these criteria.

**Table 4.1**
**Balance of Good COIN Practices and Bad COIN Practices for 30 Cases**

| Case | Good Factors (15) | Bad Factors (12) | Good – Bad Factors | Outcome |
|---|---|---|---|---|
| Afghanistan (post-Soviet) | 0 | 10 | –10 | Loss |
| Somalia | 1 | 10 | –9 | Loss |
| Chechnya I | 2 | 10 | –8 | Loss |
| Rwanda | 2 | 10 | –8 | Loss |
| Zaire (anti-Mobutu) | 0 | 8 | –8 | Loss |
| Nicaragua (Somoza) | 0 | 8 | –8 | Loss |
| Sudan (SPLA) | 2 | 9 | –7 | Loss |
| Kosovo | 1 | 8 | –7 | Loss |
| Afghanistan (anti-Soviet) | 1 | 7 | –6 | Loss |
| Papua New Guinea | 3 | 9 | –6 | Loss |
| Burundi | 2 | 8 | –6 | Loss |
| Bosnia | 1 | 6 | –5 | Loss |
| Moldova | 2 | 6 | –4 | Loss |
| Georgia/Abkhazia | 1 | 5 | –4 | Loss |
| Liberia | 3 | 7 | –4 | Loss |
| Afghanistan (Taliban) | 2 | 6 | –4 | Loss |
| Nagorno-Karabakh | 1 | 4 | –3 | Loss |
| DR Congo (anti-Kabila) | 1 | 4 | –3 | Loss |
| Tajikistan | 2 | 5 | –3 | Loss |
| Kampuchea | 1 | 3 | –2 | Loss |
| Nepal | 3 | 5 | –2 | Loss |
| Nicaragua (Contras) | 4 | 4 | 0 | Loss |
| Croatia | 8 | 3 | +5 | Win |
| Turkey (PKK) | 11 | 5 | +6 | Win |
| Uganda (ADF) | 8 | 0 | +8 | Win |
| Algeria (GIA) | 9 | 1 | +8 | Win |
| El Salvador | 12 | 2 | +10 | Win |
| Peru | 13 | 2 | +11 | Win |
| Senegal | 13 | 0 | +13 | Win |
| Sierra Leone | 14 | 1 | +13 | Win |

So, not only do good COIN practices run in packs, but where good COIN practices significantly outnumber bad COIN practices, the COIN force wins, *without exception*.

### Every Insurgency May Be Unique, but Not at This Level of Analysis

This "without exception" is particularly important, given that we are told ad nauseum that "every insurgency is unique" and, thus, every COIN must be unique.[2] This is even more remarkable given that many of the conventional explanations of the outcomes of these cases rely on a narrative of exceptionality. (That is, they list one or more distinctive or exceptional aspects of the case's history that are critical to understanding the outcome.) For example, the narrative of Turkey's 1999 triumph over the PKK indicates that victory largely hinged on the capture of the PKK's leader, Abdullah Öcalan, and on errors he had made in willfully ensuring a lack of succession for the insurgent group. Narrative accounts might further mention Turkey's failure to address the legitimate grievances of the Kurdish population and how its heavy-handed and repressive tactics had alienated the population in the area of conflict. (Our data do reflect that Turkey has the most "bad" COIN practices of any winning COIN case.) What might be given less explanatory emphasis in the narrative is the host of good COIN practices that the Turks slowly added to their approach in the later phases of the conflict. Regardless of whether the Turks would have defeated the PKK in 1999 had they not captured Öcalan, they

---

[2] Each of the following documents contains the quotation "every insurgency is unique": Joe Felter, "Taking Guns to a Knife Fight: An Empirical Study of Effective Counterinsurgency," paper presented at the annual meeting of the American Political Science Association, Philadelphia, Pa., August 31, 2006; Nagl, 2005; Sergio M. Giampietri and John H. Stone, Sr., *A Counterinsurgency Study: An Analysis of Local Defenses*, Monterey, Calif.: Naval Postgraduate School, September 2004; Raymond A. Millen, *Afghanistan: Reconstituting a Collapsed State*, Carlisle, Pa.: Strategic Studies Institute, U.S. Army War College, April 2005; Michael A. Norton, *Operational Leadership in Vietnam: General William Depuy vs. Lieutenant General Victor Krulak or Attrition Vice Pacification*, Newport, R.I.: Naval War College, May 19, 1997; Frank G. Hoffman, "Neo-Classical Counterinsurgency?" *Parameters*, Summer 2007; J. D. Harrill, *Phased Insurgency Theory: Ramadi*, Quantico, Va.: U.S. Marine Corps Command and Staff College, 2008; and Colin S. Gray, "Irregular Warfare: One Nature, Many Characters," *Strategic Studies Quarterly*, Winter 2007. Also see Appendix C.

did defeat the PKK, and at that point in the conflict, they did have a substantially positive balance of good versus bad COIN practices. No exceptions required.

So, every insurgency may be unique, but not so much that it matters at this level of analysis.[3] Our data show that, regardless of distinctiveness in the narrative and without exception, COIN forces that successfully implement preponderantly more good practices than bad win, and those that do not lose.

## Which Successful Approach Is Most Essential? Qualitative Comparative Analysis

The discovery that "good COIN practices tend to run in packs" is itself a very useful finding, but it also terribly complicates identifying which of the host of good COIN approaches is most critical or most important. To attempt to answer this question, we employed sociologist Charles Ragin's qualitative comparative analysis (QCA).[4]

QCA is particularly well suited to this application because it is designed to assess configurations of case similarities and differences using simple, logical rules. These rules run parallel to those used by researchers who conduct small-N studies (e.g., case studies with two to five cases), yet this method makes it possible to address a much larger number of cases. Using computer algorithms first developed for the simplification of switching circuits, researchers are able to compare a large number of cases as configurations, many more than they could possibly "hold in their heads" using traditional case-oriented comparative methods. As such, researchers are compelled to be explicit about

---

3 Where the distinctive features and characteristics of individual insurgencies most certainly *do* matter is in actual efforts to implement approaches and practices on the ground. Our findings do not suggest a "one size fits all" approach to COIN at the execution level; rather, these findings suggest that there is a finite set of good practices that a COIN force should always aspire to realize, but how a COIN force actually does those things in any given operation will vary depending on the context.

4 Charles C. Ragin, *The Comparative Method: Moving Beyond Qualitative and Quantitative Strategies*, Berkeley, Calif.: University of California Press, 1987.

outcomes of interest and proposed causal relations. Further, the output of the QCA process is the reduction of patterns of factors to the minimum set sufficient to explain all of the observed outcomes. Ideally, these minimally sufficient patterns would be few enough in number to tell us which of the identified COIN approaches is most essential to success in COIN. For a more detailed methodological discussion of QCA, see the section "Charles Ragin's Qualitative Comparative Analysis" in Appendix A.

So, which of the good COIN practices in the pack is most essential? Because of the co-occurrence of so many positive factors in all the COIN wins and their rarity in COIN losses, we (and QCA) were unable to make any discrimination among 16 equally plausible sets of minimally sufficient patterns of factors identified through QCA. A discussion and (fairly technical) presentation of this analysis is presented in Appendix B. A simple example of the problem would be as follows: If factor *A* and factor *B* both occur in every win and never in a loss, which is more important, *A* or *B*? Discrimination is impossible.

Ultimately, our application of QCA merely confirmed what we had already concluded from the "scorecard" analysis: Good COIN practices run in packs. The additional analysis was worthwhile, however, because in addition to confirming the previous analysis, it dismissed the possibility of interactions between multiple factors camouflaging exceptions to our existing findings. For example, the factor stacks representing every approach other than tangible support reduction fail to perfectly predict the outcome of every case; each factor stack either does not occur in at least one win or does occur in at least one loss.[5] If these factor stacks alone consistently did not predict the same wins or losses (some truly exceptional case or cases), we would not see that when comparing factors with outcomes one at a time. Both the QCA analysis and the analysis underlying the balance of good versus bad factor summation preclude the possibility of such an exceptional case. Complex patterns of different factors and approaches were evaluated relative to case outcomes, and no single pattern that was mini-

[5] Tangible support reduction's factor stack *does* perfectly predict the data; it is present in all eight COIN wins and absent in all 22 COIN losses (see Table 3.18 in Chapter Three).

mally sufficient to explain the outcome of all cases was any better than any of the others identified.

## Phase Outcomes

To accurately capture important changes during the course of these 30 insurgencies, each was broken into between two and five phases. Details of this process are described in Appendix A in the section "Phased Data." While breaking the cases into phases was useful and beneficial to the overall analysis, analyzing individual phases is problematic and minimally useful for a number of reasons. Paramount among them: We are interested in case outcomes, not phase outcomes. Understanding how to win a phase pales in comparison to understanding how to win a case, especially—as occurred repeatedly—if the COIN force managed to win a phase on the way to losing a case.

Where relevant to specific approaches, results from the analysis of the intermediate phases are presented with the approaches in Chapter Three. Our analysis of the phased data reveals a further important finding: Patterns of phase outcomes en route to wins or losses reveal success or failure in early phases, but these wins and losses do not preclude losing or winning the case. In other words, poor beginnings do not necessary lead to poor ends, and good starts do not always carry through to the end of the conflict.

With each of 30 cases having between two and five phases, there are a total of 86 phases in our dataset. Each case has a single decisive phase—that is, 30 of the 86 phases were decisive phases. The remaining 56 phases are initial or intermediate phases and illustrate the dynamic relationship between the outcomes of intermediate phases and the ultimate case outcomes. (See Table 4.2.)

Table 4.2 reveals that in more than half of the intermediate phases (nine of 16) en route to COIN wins at the case level, the insurgents held the upper hand. Similarly, in just under half (19 of 40) of intermediate phases in which the COIN force ultimately lost, the COIN force held the upper hand.

**Table 4.2**
**Phase Outcome Versus Case Outcome for 56 Intermediate Phases**

| | | Case Outcome: COIN Loss | Case Outcome: COIN Win |
|---|---|---|---|
| Phase outcome | COIN Loss | 21 | 9 |
| | COIN Win | 19 | 7 |

Of the 30 cases, nine (two COIN wins and seven COIN losses) had phase outcomes that matched the case outcome. In the other 21 cases, the side that ultimately lost the case won at least one phase. That means that in more than two-thirds of cases, the side that won did not have the upper hand in at least one phase.

CHAPTER FIVE

# Conclusions and Recommendations

This monograph employs data collected on 76 factors and three outcomes in 86 phases of the 30 most recent resolved COIN campaigns worldwide for a variety of quantitative analyses. One set of analyses tested the tenets of various approaches to COIN against the outcomes of actual COIN cases. Of the 20 (well, 21, since legitimacy is decomposed into two parts) approaches tested, 13 received strong evidentiary support, and two received some support from the evidence. We found strong evidence against three approaches (resettlement, "crush them," and insurgent support), and three could not be tested because of a lack of variance or precision in the data ("put a local face on it," cultural awareness, and amnesty).

We finish with a reprise of the key takeaways from our findings, elaborated and expanded by way of conclusions and recommendations.

## Key Findings

While Chapters Three and Four provide a host of interesting findings, we have identified those that we believe will be of greatest interest to the widest audience. Conclusions and recommendations based on each of these five key findings are discussed in turn:

- Effective COIN practices run in packs.
- The balance of good versus bad practices perfectly predicts outcomes.
- Poor beginnings do not necessarily lead to poor ends.

- Repression wins phases, but usually not cases.
- Tangible support trumps popular support.

### Effective COIN Practices Tend to Run in Packs

Of 20 approaches tested, 13 received strong evidence in these analyses (see Table 3.23 in Chapter Three). This is because we found that those who succeed in COIN do so by implementing a host of good COIN practices while avoiding adverse practices. We were unable to discern any single most important COIN practice, and the good practices all occur together (along with success) with such regularity that we cannot even rank order their importance (though we employed a method that was ideal for disentangling causal complexities). Victory, it appears, does indeed have a thousand fathers.

### The Balance of Good Versus Bad Practices Perfectly Predicts Outcomes

What is surprising is that this core finding holds across the 30 cases in our analysis *without exception*. That is, every COIN win in the data (eight of 30 cases) has a strongly positive balance of good versus detrimental factors, and every COIN loss (22 of 30 cases) has a zero or negative balance of good versus detrimental factors (see Table 4.1 in Chapter Four). This is truly remarkable given that we are told again and again that "every insurgency is unique" and, thus, every COIN must be unique. It is even *more* remarkable given that many of the conventional explanations of the outcomes of these cases rely on a narrative of exceptionality. Our data show that, regardless of distinctiveness in the narrative and without exception, COIN forces that succeed in implementing more good practices than bad win, and those that do not lose.

These two conclusions taken together lead to four recommendations, discussed in turn.

1. *Plan to pursue multiple mutually supporting lines of operation in COIN.*
2. *Build and maintain forces that are capable of engaging in multiple mutually supporting lines of operation simultaneously.*

COIN forces that prevail over insurgencies *all* register a considerable positive balance of positive practices and activities over detracting practices. Not every positive approach attempted by the COIN force will actually be successfully realized in practice. There is no hard-and-fast threshold for the minimum number of good COIN practices in which a COIN force must engage to win. The "thousand fathers" of COIN victory are not conducted in sequence, one after the other; they are conducted simultaneously. If one is serious about supporting or conducting COIN, one must be prepared to engage in as many of the identified good COIN practices as possible, for as long as necessary.

For the broader U.S. government, this means that U.S. COIN efforts must be sufficiently resourced, in terms of both staffing and other support, to give multiple areas of endeavor the attention needed. Further, non–U.S. Department of Defense (DoD) partner agencies must be made sufficiently robust to contribute to development, governance, and legitimacy, and their activities must be coordinated with DoD COIN operations. For DoD, this means rejecting out of hand any proposal or plan that emphasizes a single COIN approach or other "magic bullet" at the expense of other positive practices. Current best practices with regard to mutually supporting lines of operation from Iraq and Afghanistan must be carried forward into future contingency planning. While commanders who have served in contemporary operations intuitively accept the importance of multiple mutually supporting lines of operation to successful COIN, this intuition must be incorporated into the institutional memory of U.S. defense organizations—in joint and service doctrine both for planning and in areas specific to COIN or irregular warfare. Finally, these first two recommendations will require DoD to establish and maintain increased capabilities in the areas of building partner capacity, civil affairs and reconstruction, and information and influence operations.

3. *Ensure the positive involvement of the host-nation government.*

Several of the empirically supported approaches (e.g., democracy, government legitimacy, strategic communication) and several of the items on the list of good COIN practices or factors depend on the nature and behavior of the host-nation government. If a host-nation government or its structure and practices do not comport with good COIN practices, all possible pressure should be brought to bear to ensure government reform. Failure to realize the good COIN practices associated with government, governance, and legitimacy leaves available significantly fewer members of the pack of good COIN practices and leaves no guarantee that victory remains possible. The United States should think twice before choosing to help governments that will not help themselves.

4. *Keep a scorecard of good versus bad factors and practices; if the balance does not correspond to the desired outcome, make changes.*

Table 4.1 in Chapter Four showed that, without exception, winning COIN forces had a significant positive balance of good practices relative to bad practices, and losing COIN forces had a zero or negative balance. When engaging in COIN operations, as dispassionately and accurately as possible, assess the presence or absence of the good and bad factors listed in Chapter Four, and add them up. Is the COIN force where it should be (remembering that the lowest-scoring COIN winner had a balance of five)? If not, change strategies (or implementation). A blank scorecard can be found at the end of this volume.

This recommendation applies to both the commanders in charge of operations and the senior civilian leadership responsible for strategies and resources. The balance of the 15 good and 12 bad practices or factors identified (and historically validated) here should be added to other progress or status metrics currently in use.

### Poor Beginnings Do Not Necessarily Lead to Poor Ends

These analyses show that getting off to a poor start in the early phases of a conflict does not necessarily lead to a COIN loss. Of the eight cases won by the COIN force, in only two cases were the outcomes of all phases favorable to the COIN force. In fact, in three of the cases won by the COIN force, the COIN force had the upper hand only in the decisive phase. Changing practices can lead to changed outcomes.

5. *Recognize that there is time to adapt.*

Obviously, it would be better to start with and stick with good COIN practices, but that is sometimes easier said than done, especially when working by, with, or through partner-nation forces. Just because a COIN or COIN-support operation gets off to a seemingly poor start, do not abandon the intention of following good COIN practices. Of the eight winning COIN forces in our case studies, only two (Senegal and Croatia) won every phase of the conflict. Three of the winners (Peru, Sierra Leone, and Uganda) won only the final phase. Getting off to a bad start does not doom a COIN operation. Recognize that providing support for a struggling COIN operation or reinvesting in a failing one is not a strategically quixotic or doomed endeavor.

For DoD, our fifth recommendation has important implications for balancing risk. If future scenarios include the possibility of major combat operations against a peer or near-peer adversary, failure to adequately program for such a contingency is an unacceptable risk. Loss in such a conflict could be unbearably costly for the nation. If futures include COIN operations (and any plausible future must), the risk associated with being insufficiently prepared for such operations is lower: COIN operations may face initial setbacks and may take longer to see ultimate resolution, but initial failure does not necessitate ultimate failure—there is time to adapt. Risk calculation–based allocations must be mindful not only of the relatively greater likelihood of COIN operations than major combat operations against near-peer adversaries but also of the relatively lower levels of risk associated with initial shortcomings in the former.

### Repression Wins Phases, but Usually Not Cases

While some repressive COIN forces have managed to prevail, this analysis shows unambiguously that repression is a bad COIN practice. Only two of eight COIN winners used repression, and they still employed a pack of good COIN practices—apparently enough to offset the negative impact of repression. Repression does win phases, but, in our data, the vast majority of phases won with repression preceded ultimate defeat in the case. Consider the case of Tajikistan in the mid-

1990s. The Tajik government and its Russian allies aggressively and indiscriminately smashed back against an initially successful insurgency, temporarily gaining the upper hand but further alienating the population by ignoring its needs, grievances, and well-being. Repression can win phases by dealing the insurgents a blow and making support for them more costly, but our data show that the vast majority of phases that were won with repression ultimately increased popular support for the insurgency and ended in a COIN defeat for the entire case. While it is possible to find examples of success in COIN through repression, they are either exceptions or short-term victories.

6. *Avoid using and discourage allies and partners from using repression and collective punishment in COIN.*

U.S. military doctrine and practice preclude the use of disproportionate force or collective punishment, so this is not a concern with regard to U.S. forces. However, all possible partners and allies do not share this prohibition. When joining allies or establishing or reestablishing partner security forces (or militias), all possible care should be taken to ensure that they maintain proper respect for human rights and have a full understanding of the likely long-term consequences of routine disproportionate or illegitimate uses of force. If partners are unlikely to adhere to these standards, they should be avoided as partners.

### Tangible Support Trumps Popular Support

The ability of insurgents to replenish and obtain personnel, materiel, financing, intelligence, and sanctuary (tangible support) perfectly predicts success or failure in the 30 COIN cases considered here. In all eight cases in which the COIN force prevailed, it also disrupted at least three insurgent support factors, while none of the COIN forces in the 22 losing cases managed to disrupt more than two. When support comes primarily from the population, then popular support is the center of gravity. However, when popular support and tangible support diverged in our data (i.e., the insurgents did not have the support of the population but did have their support needs met by some set of external actors), tangible support proved more important. This suggests an important caveat to population-centric COIN approaches: The population is the center of gravity if the population is the primary source of tangible insurgent support.

7. *Ascertain the specific support needs of and sources of support for insurgent adversaries and target them.*

When insurgents draw their support primarily from the population, a primarily population-focused set of COIN strategies should work. When insurgents' support comes from external actors (or other sources), then approaches explicitly targeting that supply chain are necessary, along with efforts to win over the population. (Victory still has a thousand fathers, so do not expect to win just by interdicting insurgents' tangible support.) DoD should ensure that this strategic and operational imperative is prominent in future plans and doctrine.

APPENDIX A

# Methods and Data

This appendix describes the overall methodological approach employed in this research, the historical COIN cases informing the analyses and how they were selected, and the specific methods used in the analyses. Our goal for these analyses was to test the validity and range of applicability of the 20 approaches to COIN described in Chapter Three against substantial historical evidence. How have those who have adhered to the tenets of various COIN approaches fared historically? How can these lessons inform preparations for contemporary and future COIN contingencies?

## Charles Ragin's Qualitative Comparative Analysis

Early in our research planning, we remembered a previous encounter with sociologist Charles Ragin's work on case-based comparative historical analysis using QCA, a tool designed to assess configurations of case similarities and differences using simple logical rules.[1] We carefully considered the application of his methods to this problem and concluded that QCA was an ideal match. We structured our data collection and analysis to allow us to employ Ragin's QCA approach.

Through the use of "truth tables," QCA provides a holistic approach to qualitative historical comparison by viewing cases in terms

[1] See Ragin, 1987.

of combinations of binary (present or absent) factors.[2] Using computer algorithms first developed for the simplification of switching circuits, researchers are able to compare a large number of cases as configurations, many more than they could possibly hold in their heads using traditional case-oriented comparative methods. This case-based method for analytic aggregation allows for the quantification of otherwise voluminous amounts of qualitative data. As such, it compels researchers to be explicit about outcomes of interest and proposed causal relations, including necessary or sufficient causes and conditional or contributing causes.

QCA relies on the application of Boolean algebra to a truth table, in which selected factors are scored as present or absent (1 or 0) for all selected cases.[3] The truth table has as many rows as there are logically possible combinations of values for the selected factors. (For example, including four binary factors in the analysis would result in $2^4 = 2 \times 2 \times 2 \times 2 = 16$ rows.) Rows are first reduced by removing patterns of factors that do not occur in the data—that is, any row that does not correspond to one or more actual cases. Boolean algebra then allows further reduction of the combinatorial matrix to expose simplified patterns of relationships and determine the prime implicants.

Prime implicants are the minimally sufficient patterns of factors that fully describe the pattern of outcomes of a set of cases. In our analysis, approaches (or patterns of factors representing approaches)

---

2 *Binary* indicates that a factor can take on only one of two values. In our case, that is *present* or *absent*, always represented by 1 and 0, respectively. A truth table, then, is a collection of rows of 1s and 0s that represent every pattern of presence and absence of the factors of interest that appear in the data.

3 Boolean algebra was developed in 1954 by George Boole. (See George Boole, *An Investigation of the Laws of Thought*, Amherst, N.Y.: Prometheus, 2003.) Boolean algebra differs from standard high school algebra in two ways. First, values are logical values instead of numerical values. These are *true* or *false*, *present* or *absent*, and are represented as 1 or 0. Second, logical values dictate slightly different mathematical operations obeying slightly different mathematical laws. Many readers will be familiar with Boolean search operators, such as *and*, *or*, and *not*, as they can be used in some search engines. The application of Boolean algebra here has two implications: It requires us to structure our data with logical values (true or false, or, in our case, present or absent), and it allows complex patterns of data to be reduced to the minimum set of factors necessary to determine a pattern, called *prime implicants*.

that can be shown to be prime implicants describing the patterns of success or failure (the outcomes) in our cases receive strong support.

Though the prime implicants are determined through a logical reduction of quantitative data, once they are identified, the analysis can turn back to the qualitative nuance of the cases. Cases in which surprising patterns occur, or in which patterns that usually result in success do not, can be singled out for more detailed case-study analysis. This can lead to further inductive theory development. Imagine a situation in which the presence of three factors leads to a COIN force win in all cases except one. Thorough and careful examination of the details of that exceptional case could reveal many different things, any of which would be informative. It could be that one or more of the three critical factors are not really present in the exceptional case, but they were evaluated as present based on a superficial reading of the history, which a detailed review exposes as incorrect. Or, it could be that the three critical factors are very much present, but a detailed exploration of the case reveals a narrative showing that the impact of the three factors is thwarted by the presence of a fourth factor, which proves to be absent in the other cases containing the original three factors of concern. In this event, the addition of a fourth factor perfects the set of prime implicants. (Now, the presence of three factors plus the absence of the new fourth perfectly predicts COIN force victory.) Discerning what exactly is exceptional about the exceptional case leads to a better understanding of that case and of the other cases as well.

This method is particularly well suited to our research effort because it allows mathematical principles to be applied to fundamentally qualitative data without in any way compromising the qualitative nuance necessary to identify and resolve exceptions. Boolean reduction allows us to identify and evidence factors and interactions between factors that have historically led to successful COIN outcomes. Thus, we can test the approaches associated with these factors.

In many cases, the intention to apply QCA drove how we structured our data and the collection of those data. For a more in-depth explanation of how QCA was actually applied to these data, see the section "Additional Details on the Use of Ragin's QCA," later in this appendix.

## Case Selection

QCA is potentially applicable across any set of cases. As is true with any inferential analyses, findings are generalizable only across cases that can be argued to be comparable with the sampled cases. Since our sponsor's interests focus on preparing U.S. forces for success in contemporary and future operations, we sought historical cases that were likely to be as representative as possible of the contemporary state of the art in insurgency and COIN. We elected to study the world's 30 most recent resolved COIN campaigns. We chose to conduct 30 case studies based on the amount of detail required for each case and the time and resources available; we chose completed cases because we were interested in factors that contributed to the outcome, which are impossible to assess if the outcome is not yet determined. Once we had compiled a list of the world's resolved insurgencies, we chose those with the most recent start dates as mostly likely to be like current and future cases.

Identifying and enumerating historical insurgencies worldwide is a nontrivial undertaking. There have been many insurgencies in the course of human history and many other similar conflicts from which they must be distinguished.[4] RAND's Martin Libicki recently prepared a list of 20th- and 21st-century insurgencies.[5] He began with a list of 127 insurgencies started by 1999 that was developed by other scholars.[6] These 127 cases met three criteria:

- They involved fighting between states and nonstates seeking to take control of a government or region or that used violence to attempt to change government policies.
- The conflict killed at least 1,000 people over its course, with a yearly average of at least 100.

---

[4] Insurgency is a centuries old form of conflict that pits the weak against the strong. Indeed, writing between 400 and 300 B.C, with an emphasis on intelligence, hit-and-run tactics, and adaptability, Chinese strategist Sun Tzu essentially laid out the basis of guerrilla warfare in his timeless classic *The Art of War*. Ancient Rome also provided fertile ground for insurgency in such places as Gaul and Judaea.

[5] Libicki, 2008.

[6] The base list comes from Fearon and Laitin, 2003.

- At least 100 people were killed on both sides (including civilians attacked by rebels).

Starting with this list, Libicki first excluded cases that could be classified as coups, countercoups, or insurrections. (There were 51 such cases; subtracted from 127, this leaves 76.) He then added 11 insurgencies that began (or crossed the threshold of 1,000 deaths) after the 1999 cutoff of the foundational list (so, 87 cases). Finally, careful consideration led two conflicts that had previously been excluded to be returned to the list. This left 89 insurgencies covering the period from 1934 to 2008.

For this research, we selected the 30 most recent resolved cases from Libicki's list. These 30 cases also correspond to a 30-year chronological span: All the insurgencies began and ended between 1978 and 2008. Table A.1 lists the 30 insurgencies used for our case studies.

**Table A.1**
**Countries, Insurgents, and Date Spans of the 30 Case-Study Insurgencies**

| Country (Insurgency) | Years | Outcome |
|---|---|---|
| Nicaragua (Somoza) | 1978–1979 | COIN loss |
| Afghanistan (anti-Soviet) | 1978–1992 | COIN loss |
| Kampuchea | 1978–1992 | COIN loss |
| El Salvador | 1979–1992 | **COIN win** |
| Somalia | 1980–1991 | COIN loss |
| Peru | 1980–1992 | **COIN win** |
| Nicaragua (Contras) | 1981–1990 | COIN loss |
| Senegal | 1982–2002 | **COIN win** |
| Turkey (PKK) | 1984–1999 | **COIN win** |
| Sudan (SPLA) | 1984–2004 | COIN loss |
| Uganda (ADF) | 1986–2000 | **COIN win** |
| Papua New Guinea | 1988–1998 | COIN loss |
| Liberia | 1989–1997 | COIN loss |
| Rwanda | 1990–1994 | COIN loss |
| Moldova | 1990–1992 | COIN loss |
| Sierra Leone | 1991–2002 | **COIN win** |

**Table A.1—Continued**

| Country (Insurgency) | Years | Outcome |
|---|---|---|
| Algeria (GIA) | 1992–2004 | **COIN win** |
| Croatia | 1992–1995 | **COIN win** |
| Afghanistan (post-Soviet) | 1992–1996 | COIN loss |
| Tajikistan | 1992–1997 | COIN loss |
| Georgia/Abkhazia | 1992–1994 | COIN loss |
| Nagorno-Karabakh | 1992–1994 | COIN loss |
| Bosnia | 1992–1995 | COIN loss |
| Burundi | 1993–2003 | COIN loss |
| Chechnya I | 1994–1996 | COIN loss |
| Afghanistan (Taliban) | 1996–2001 | COIN loss |
| Zaire (anti-Mobutu) | 1996–1997 | COIN loss |
| Kosovo | 1978–1979 | COIN loss |
| Nepal | 1978–1992 | COIN loss |
| DR Congo (anti-Kabila) | 1978–1992 | COIN loss |

NOTE: "COIN loss" includes the outcomes "insurgent win" and "mixed, favoring insurgents" (nine of 22 case losses were mixed outcomes favoring the insurgents). "COIN win" includes "COIN win" and "mixed, favoring COIN force." "Mixed, favoring COIN force" occurs only once in the eight COIN wins. For details on outcome scoring and categories, see the section "Outcome Assessment," later in this appendix.

This set of cases has many attractive features from an analytical perspective. First, it is exhaustive over the period under examination, and so it constitutes the whole universe of insurgencies begun and resolved between 1978 and 2008. This is not a sample of insurgencies over this period—this is the whole population. No statistics are necessary to make inferences about the extent to which these data represent a larger population; the data are perfectly representative of the past 30 years of completed COIN operations. Second, all 30 insurgencies fall after the dawn of television news, so they account for at least some of the striking changes in the global media environment in recent history. Third, in none of the cases is the United States the principal counterinsurgent actor.[7] This facilitates open-minded comparisons for U.S. audiences between the way U.S. forces have and might yet undertake COIN operations and the way others have done so.[8] Fourth, they represent many different regions, with cases in South America, Central Asia, Africa, and the Far East. If regional differences in the conduct or context of COIN were to significantly affect the performance of various approaches to COIN, these data would reflect them.

## Factor Generation, Evaluation, and Scoring

For each case, we completed a case narrative and collected data on 76 specific factors.[9] Selecting the factors to evaluate was itself a methodologically interesting process.

Crisp-set QCA requires binary data for reduction to prime implicants using Boolean algebra. Given the difficulty of trying to quantify many of the concepts central to the approaches we sought to test (e.g., security, democracy, legitimacy) in any discrete, scaled, or even ordinal way, binary (present/absent, 1/0) scoring was eminently suitable.

The identification and refinement of these binary factors was an inductive and iterative process. We began with an extensive review of the literature on strategic communication and COIN, from which we selected the 20 approaches offered as explanatory variables in these

---

7 The United States was involved in several cases in an advisory role or as a contributor of materiel support to one side or the other. In several cases, the United States contributed significant military forces (e.g., Kosovo, Afghanistan), but, in those cases, the United States and its NATO allies were technically on the side of the insurgents. The United States also supported the insurgents in both Nicaragua cases.

8 For possible disadvantages attendant to this set of cases, see Appendix C.

9 While 76 (plus three outcomes) is the number of factors used in our analyses and presented here, we actually collected (or attempted to collect) data on numerous additional factors. These factors are not included here because either (1) they proved impossible to ascertain in many of the cases or (2) they proved to be of no analytical value. Factors in the latter category were not explicitly associated with one of the 20 approaches to COIN that we were testing, but they were factors drawn from our experience researching conflict flashpoints (see Paul et al., 2008) or identified inductively as factors that appeared significant in the developing case narratives early in the research process.

analyses and presented in Chapter Three. For each approach, we distilled a set of core tenets (also presented in Chapter Three). Based on these tenets, we identified sets of discrete, measureable factors (also listed in Chapter Three) to represent each approach and to be indentified as present or absent in each case.

Once we identified the practices advocated by the various COIN approaches and laid them out as measurable factors, we engaged in vigorous debate over whether the factors truly represented what we intended them to capture. We revisited the factor list repeatedly as data collection and analysis progressed. This process of refinement spanned much of the project and relied on examples and experiences from the individual case studies as well as from COIN cases not included in this analysis but with which we were familiar. Factors were adjusted (or eliminated) due to the difficulty of assessing them with the available historical data, because of the nuance necessary for specific cases, or to better capture the tenets of the approaches as they played out in real cases. Whenever a factor or its criteria were changed, all previously scored data on that factor were reviewed for consistency with the change (this occurred across all phases).

For example, several of our preliminary factors were dropped for being too difficult to measure against the historical record. These included "Messages consistent (or at least progressive) over time" in the realm of strategic communication and "COIN force employed ID cards/checkpoints for population control." Other factors were changed subtly to make them either easier to assess or more representative of the tenets. For example, "Leaders selected in a manner considered just and fair by majority of population" became "Government leaders selected in a manner considered just and fair by majority of population in area of conflict." "COIN forces attempted to secure border(s)" became "Flow of cross-border insurgent support significantly decreased or remained dramatically reduced or largely absent."

In addition to factors derived from specific COIN approaches and inductively revised based on experience with the actual data, we also included factors induced from the cases. As we conducted the case studies, the preliminary narratives suggested other factors that appeared to be making important contributions to determining case outcomes. After some discussion, we added these inductive factors to our factor list if they could not be explained away through reference to other factors.

The 76 factors that represent the specific approaches used in the analysis are presented in Chapter Three, along with a discussion of each approach. The 57 factors that are tied to a specific approach are also listed in the matrix at the end of this volume. We also included 19 additional factors that are not explicitly tied to an approach:

- The COIN force engaged in more coercion or intimidation than the insurgents.
- The insurgents were delegitimized through civilian casualties or other unacceptable behavior.
- The security of the population in the area of conflict improved from the previous phase.
- There was external support to COIN from a strong state or military.
- There was external support to the insurgents from a strong state or military.
- An external professional military engaged in fighting on behalf of the government.
- An external professional military engaged in fighting on behalf of the insurgents.
- The COIN force (and allies) and insurgents (and allies) *lacked* sophisticated modern military equipment and vehicles.
- The COIN force (and allies) had significant military equipment mismatch dominance over the insurgents (and allies).
- The COIN force had and used uncontested air dominance.
- The COIN force had air superiority, but use of airspace was significantly contested or the COIN force was unable take advantage of air power.
- The COIN force was of sufficient strength to force the insurgents to fight as guerrillas.
- The insurgent force was individually superior to the COIN force by being either more professional or better motivated.
- The COIN force or allies relied on looting for sustainment.

- The COIN force and government had different goals/levels of commitment.
- The government or state was competent.
- COIN or insurgent actions precipitated (or constituted) ethnic or religious violence.
- There were expropriable cash crops or mineral wealth in the area of conflict.
- The phase was the decisive (probably terminal, but not necessarily) phase of the case.

All 76 factors and three outcome possibilities were scored as present or absent (1 or 0) for each case based on the best assessment of the analyst responsible for that case. To ensure consistency in criteria for evaluating the presence or absence of each factor, the research team met regularly to discuss factor assignments. Each project team member was responsible for a subset of the cases. Each analyst worked on between six and 12 cases concurrently, so all had ample examples on which to draw to illustrate a point, highlight a challenge to discrimination, or test candidate criteria language. We discussed factors and criteria to ensure shared understanding, and we collectively examined the details of difficult or borderline cases for certain factors. This exchange of concrete examples and counterexamples resulted in either new consensus on and understanding of existing criteria or revision to the factor's wording or criteria.

### Outcome Assessment

The step that was most critical to the results of the analysis was the assessment of the outcome of each case. Unsurprisingly, since we do not live in a dichotomous world, some of the case outcomes were somewhat ambiguous. Libicki, in the 89 cases from which we chose the most recent 30, had provisional outcomes for each case as assessed by his research team, and many of them were "mixed." While we retained "mixed" outcome as a factor in the data, we knew that we wanted a discrete binary outcome for our core analyses. In other words, "mixed" was not good enough. For each case with a mixed outcome, the case analyst made a determination of "mixed, favoring the COIN force" or "mixed, favoring the insurgents." In no case was the outcome so truly ambiguous that the result could not be clearly identified as favoring one party or the other. This became especially clear once the cases were broken down into phases. In all analyses, unless otherwise specified, "mixed, favoring the COIN force" is included in "COIN win" and "mixed, favoring the insurgents" is included in "COIN loss."

To adjudicate unclear case outcomes, we followed the logic illustrated in Figure A.1. First, for each case, we asked whether the government against which the insurgency arose had stayed in power through the end of the conflict and whether it retained sovereignty over the region of conflict. If insurgents either deposed (or otherwise led to the fall of) the government or won de facto control of a separatist region, then the COIN force did *not* win. If the government remained in power and the country intact, then we further considered whether the government had been forced (or chose) to make major concessions to the insurgents, such as power sharing in government or loss of territory or other sovereign control, or was otherwise forced to yield to insurgent demands. If the government stayed in power, the country remained intact, and no major concessions were granted to the insurgents, then the COIN force unambiguously won. If, however, major concessions were made, then the outcome was mixed. In all cases, what constituted a "major" concession and who (the COIN force or the insurgents) had the better of a mixed outcome was decided at the discretion of the individual case analyst based on the distinct narrative of that case.

## *p* and (1 – *p*)

As noted, all factors were scored as present or absent, 1 or 0, for each case. Some of the factors are described as negations; for example, one factor is "COIN force *not* viewed as an occupying force in area of conflict." If this factor is scored present (1) for a case, that means that the

**Figure A.1**
**Logic for Assignment of Case Outcomes**

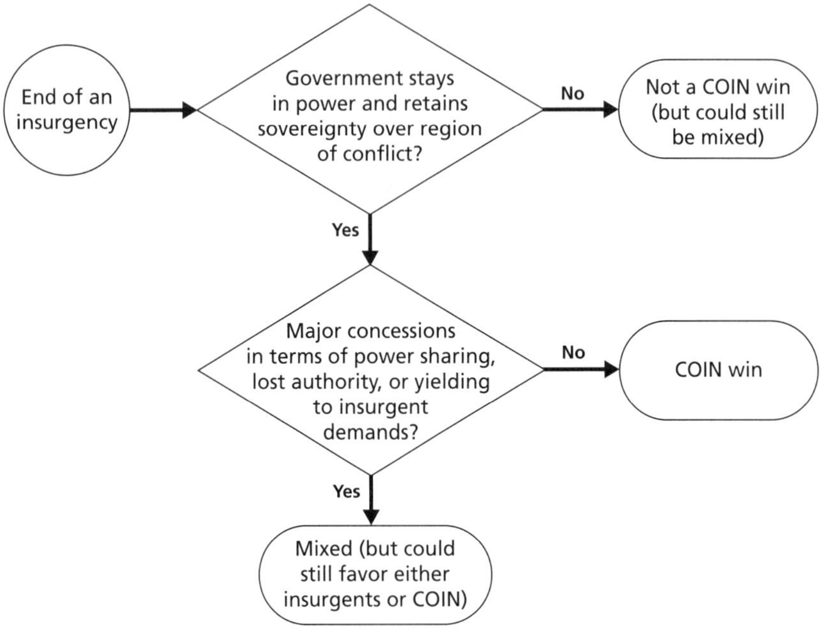


RAND *MG964-A.1*

COIN force was not viewed as an occupying force in the area of conflict. This follows standard practice for dummy or indicator variables and also adheres to English-language conventions regarding double negatives.

Some of the analyses focused on the presence of certain factors, while others focused on the absence of those factors. (Specifically, our analysis of good COIN practices focused on the presence of those good practices, while our analysis of detrimental COIN practices usually identified a poor practice as the absence of an otherwise positive factor.) While leaving the underlying data intact, we avoid double negatives throughout the discussion and presentation of the findings to the extent possible. We do this by invoking the relationship between a probability $p$ and $(1 - p)$. Consider factors in which $p$ is either 1 or 0 (as is the case for all our factor scores): $(1 - p)$ will always be the other of 1 or 0. So, if a case is scored 0 for "COIN force *not* viewed as an occupying force in the area of conflict," that means that it is *not* not viewed as an occupier, which means that it *is* viewed as an occupier. We avoid awkward double negatives by describing the obverse factor rather than the negation of the factor; in this example, we would simply say, "COIN force viewed as an occupying force in the area of conflict," if that were the relationship of interest.

## Data Collection

Data for the case studies (both narrative and factor evaluation) came from secondary sources. The analyst assigned to each case thoroughly reviewed the available English-language history and secondary analysis of the conflict for that case. Documentation proved voluminous for some cases (particularly those in Central and South America but also cases in which Russian or Soviet forces were involved); it was much more sparse for other cases (particularly those in Africa). In all cases, available information was sufficient to meet our data needs.

### Phased Data

We initially set out to score factors for the decisive phase of each case. Many of these cases lasted ten or more years and saw many different strategies employed by the government and the insurgents, as well as significant wholesale changes in exogenous factors that could be relevant to the outcome. By focusing on the factors present or absent at or immediately prior to the point of decision for the case, we hoped to capture the conditions that led to the observed outcome. Throughout this discussion, *case data* refers to the data for the decisive phase of the case.

We intentionally sought data for the decisive phase rather than the terminal phase because the two did not match in all cases. In three of the 30 cases, the decisive phase preceded the terminal phase: Afghanistan (anti-Soviet), Papua New Guinea, and Nagorno-Karabakh (see the accompanying volume, *Victory Has a Thousand Fathers: Detailed Counterinsurgency Case Studies*, for further details). A single example is instructive. The insurgency in Nagorno-Karabakh followed an interesting path. In the initial phase, the Karabakh Armenian insurgency made modest headway against the government. In the second phase, the Russians provided heavy weapons to both sides, but the more disciplined insurgents took advantage of political discord in the government to seize the initiative and occupy and control the majority of the territory in their declared separatist region. In the third and final phase, the COIN force reorganized and put significant pressure on the insurgents, beginning to roll them back with a series of stinging victories. However, before the government could press its advantage, the Russians put irresistible pressure on both sides for an immediate settlement, "freezing" the conflict with the insurgents still in de facto control of much of the territory they sought. Because of this peculiar close to the terminal phase, the second phase became the decisive phase; the factors changed in the third phase and did not have any effect on the outcome.

Due to the kinds of complexity that the Nagorno-Karabakh example illustrates, we ultimately separated each COIN case into two to five phases. While our core analyses still focus on the decisive phase, collecting data for all phases helped us avoid several pitfalls.

First, it seemed like a critical omission to summarize a case in a single row, with factors scored as present or absent that had not been present or absent for the majority of the conflict but were at the point of resolution. Second, those of us with backgrounds in comparative historical narrative research understood the possible importance of sequence in historical outcomes, a possibility we were ignoring by reducing our cases to a single row. The phased record for the whole case accurately reflects the condition of all factors throughout the conflict, not just in the decisive phase.

Identifying phase durations and break points proved to be at least as much art as science. Phases are not of uniform duration. A new phase was declared when the case analyst recognized a significant shift in the COIN approach, in the approach of the insurgents, or in the exogenous conditions of the case that caused changes in the assessment of several factors. Phases were *not* intended to capture microchanges or tiny cycles of adaptation and counteradaptation between the insurgents and the COIN force; rather, these were macro-level and sea-change phases. Case analysts had discretion regarding the number of phases and the number of factors that needed to change to constitute a phase change. As with the individual factors, phase breaks were discussed during team meetings to ensure comparability across cases. Secondary analysis of the cases often helped, as other analysts would include periods or phases in their narratives. Similarly, elections resulting in a change in government, or the entrance or exit of an important external participant in the conflict, were often clear indicators of phase change.

### Challenges to Analyzing Phased Data

As Chapters Three and Four showed, the phased data provided some very interesting findings. These data are fundamentally quite challenging to analyze, however. First, the phases are not independent; that is, each phase of a case is part of a sequence and has a strong relationship with the phases before and after it. Most statistical techniques assume independence of cases, which we do not have if we consider all 86 phases in the data together.

Second, the outcomes of phases other than the decisive phase of a case are mere curiosities. While it is interesting to see what types of practices and patterns of factors correlate with winning a phase in a COIN operation, we are really only interested in which factors and practices determine the ultimate outcome of the operation.

Third, similar to the challenge of discriminating the case outcome when the outcome is mixed, phase outcomes are even more problematic. For each phase, the case analyst determined whether the COIN force or the insurgents had the upper hand based on the apparent narrative trajectory at the end of the phase. Assessment of the phase outcome for other than the decisive phase was partially counterfactual (Who *would* have won if things went on as they were?) and partly speculative.

These difficulties aside, some interesting analyses are possible with the phased data. Although intermediate outcomes are not particularly interesting, intermediate outcomes relative to final outcomes *are*. For each phase, we established one of four case referential outcomes:

1. COIN force phase loss in a case it ultimately lost
2. COIN force phase loss in a case it ultimately won
3. COIN force phase win in a case it ultimately lost
4. COIN force phase win in a case it ultimately won.

The second and third outcomes are clearly the most interesting. We conducted the same bivariate analyses described later in this appendix for the phase case referential outcomes as well as for the case-level outcomes. The most interesting of the results are presented in Chapters Three and Four.

## Analyses

Using these data, we conducted three different types of analysis. The first was a brief narrative for each case, presented in the accompanying volume, *Victory Has a Thousand Fathers: Detailed Counterinsurgency Case Studies*.[10] This is also where the factor data for each phase of each case can be found. The second was a bivariate analysis of factors or approaches and cases or phases. Results from these analyses are presented in Chapter Three. The third was QCA, as described at the beginning of this appendix. The QCA results are presented in Chapter Four; a detailed presentation of that analysis is in Appendix B.

### Narratives

To give context to the raw phased factor data, we developed a brief narrative for each case. Each narrative includes a short summary of the case, a brief summary of each phase, a discussion of the conventional explanations of the case offered in the existing secondary analysis, and a list of distinct factors that were either uncommon but present in that case or wholly unique to that case.

Beyond this, we offer no separate analysis of the individual cases. In fact, one of the most striking findings of this research is that we do not need to discuss any of the distinct features or narrative peculiari-

[10] Paul, Clarke, and Grill, 2010.

ties of the individual cases to wholly explain the outcomes. Unlike in our other research efforts, here, we are not relying on narrative historical methods to reach our conclusions.[11] In fact, our analysis supports the idea that it is a mistake to learn too many "lessons" from a single case, as the peculiarities and distinctions of a single case may obfuscate otherwise critical and enduring relationships between COIN practices and outcomes.

### Bivariate Relationships

Our quantitative analysis began by identifying simple bivariate relationships between the various factors and the outcome of the case (or phase).[12] We computed bivariate correlations for all factors and case outcome and also created 2×2 tables for each factor and the case outcome. These 2×2 tables provided particularly interesting results, especially when the "diagonal" cells contained small values or were zeroes, indicating a very strong degree of association between the factor and the outcome.

Table A.2 shows, for example, that in all five cases in which the COIN force maintained credibility with the population in the area of conflict, the COIN force prevails.

As is always the case with bivariate displays, no effort is made to control for the presence or absence of other factors. Thus, while Table A.2 suggests that maintaining credibility is a good COIN practice, it tells us nothing about the other things those victorious COIN forces were or were not doing.

---

[11] For various discussions of narrative historical methods, see Andrew Abbott, "Conceptions of Time and Events in Social Science Methods: Causal and Narrative Approaches," *Historical Methods*, Vol. 23, No. 4, 1990; Ronald Aminzade, "Historical Sociology and Time," *Sociological Methods and Research*, Vol. 20, No. 4, 1992; and Robin Stryker, "Beyond History Versus Theory: Strategic Narrative and Sociological Explanation," *Sociological Methods and Research*, Vol. 24, No. 3, 1996.

[12] *Bivariate analysis* denotes consideration of the relationship between two variables. In these analyses, that is always some factor (or stack of factors representing an approach combined into a single factor) considered in relationship to the outcome of the phase or case.

**Table A.2**
**Sample 2×2 Table: COIN Force Credibility Versus Case Outcome**

| COIN force maintained credibility with population in area of conflict (includes expectation management) | | Case Outcome: COIN Loss | Case Outcome: COIN Win |
|---|---|---|---|
| | 1 (present) | 0 | 5 |
| | 0 (absent) | 22 | 3 |

Because our cases fully represent our population (we have the complete set of resolved insurgencies from 1978–2008), we do not compute inference statistics (e.g., $\chi^2$ tests, p-values) for any of our analyses. The relationships observed are perfectly representative of the relationships in this population of cases.

### Factor Stacks

We also sought to examine the bivariate relationships between the 20 approaches to COIN presented in Chapter Three and the phase and case outcomes. Because each approach is represented by more than one factor (see Chapter Four for the detailed breakdown of the factors for each approach), we faced a challenging question: How many of the factors associated with a given approach to COIN must have been present in a case before the COIN force is considered to have applied that approach? Rather than attempting to answer this question in an abstract or arbitrary way, we let the data speak and sought the best empirical cut point for each approach.

For each COIN approach, we created a new factor or variable that was the sum of all the factors tied to that approach and present in a given phase or case. We then chose a threshold value for that sum that maximized the number of COIN wins associated with the approach and minimized the number of COIN losses. Here is a concrete example: Strategic communication as a COIN approach is represented in the data by seven discrete factors (see Chapter Three). For each case, we summed these seven factors, creating a new variable, "sum of strategic communication factors." The results are shown in Table A.3.

Here, the empirical cut point is clearly at two or more. Having at least two strategic communication factors captures all eight COIN wins and excludes all but two COIN losses. Thus, we created a single variable to represent strategic communication in the analysis: "at least two strategic communication factors," scored present or absent (1 or 0) like all the other factors in the analysis.

We created a "factor stack" for each of the 20 approaches that we tested. These single factor stacks were used to represent each of the approaches in both the bivariate and qualitative comparative analyses. We also used the intermediate stage, the sum of factors, to combine and compare "good" practices and factors with "bad" factors (see Table 4.1 in Chapter Four).

### Additional Details on the Use of Ragin's QCA

As indicated at the beginning of this appendix, we structured our data to facilitate the application of Ragin's QCA approach. The construction of crisp-set truth tables requires that all data be binary, hence our

**Table A.3**
**Sum of Strategic Communication Factors Versus Case Outcome (empirical cut point in red)**

| Sum of strategic communication factors | Case Outcome: COIN Loss | Case Outcome: COIN Win |
|---|---|---|
| 7 | 0 | 1 |
| 6 | 0 | 2 |
| 5 | 0 | 1 |
| 4 | 0 | 0 |
| 3 | 1 | 4 |
| 2 | 1 | 4 |
| 1 | 5 | 0 |
| 0 | 15 | 0 |

efforts to reduce all factors and approaches to present or absent (1 or 0). For the actual analysis, we used Ragin's fsQCA (fuzzy-set QCA) software.[13] We used the crisp-set option in fsQCA to analyze our data.[14]

A wholly atheoretical data-mining approach would have encouraged us to take all 76 of our factors, enter them into a truth table, and allow Ragin's software to reduce them to prime implicants using Boolean algebra. While this might have exposed unexpected and interesting patterns in the data, it also would have increased our vulnerability to Type I error.[15] In any event, this proved impossible. A truth table has a number of possible rows equal to $2^n$, where $n$ is equal to the number of factors included. Including all 76 factors would have required a table with $2^{76}$ rows, a mind-blowing matrix size, but, more importantly, a computer-blowing one as well. The intersection of computational demand for Boolean processing and processor capacity available limited us to the inclusion of no more than 11 factors at a time (so, a truth table of $2^{11}$ possible combinations, or 2,048 unique rows).

Based on our preliminary bivariate analyses of the case data, we entered composite factors representing the 12 COIN approaches that received strong support at the bivariate level into fsQCA.[16] To ensure that we identified as many of the prime implicant patterns of these 12 composite factors as possible, we ran fsQCA analyses repeatedly, iteratively removing and replacing a factor each time we identified a prime implicant pattern. We iterated through composite elements of

---

[13] Charles C. Ragin, Kriss A. Drass, and Sean Davey, *Fuzzy-Set/Qualitative Comparative Analysis 2.0*, Tucson, Ariz.: Department of Sociology, University of Arizona, 2006. See also Charles C. Ragin, *User's Guide to Fuzzy-Set/Qualitative Comparative Analysis 2.0*, Tucson, Ariz.: Department of Sociology, University of Arizona, 2006.

[14] For the distinction between fuzzy sets and crisp sets, see Charles C. Ragin, *Fuzzy-Set Social Science*, Chicago, Ill.: University of Chicago Press, 2000.

[15] Type I error is rejecting the null hypothesis when the null hypothesis is true. That is, asserting a finding when in fact what you have found is strictly the result of chance. This is a frequent problem in data mining. See Egon S. Pearson and Jerzy Neyman, "On the Problem of Two Samples," in Jerzy Neyman and Egon S. Pearson, *Joint Statistical Papers*, Cambridge, UK: Cambridge University Press, [1930] 1967.

[16] Chapter Four reveals that 13 approaches received strong support. One of them, however, "continuation and contestation," is an insurgent-side approach. We exclude it from the QCA because our emphasis is on successful practices for COIN forces.

each set of prime implicants, slowly removing factors whose role as part of a prime implicant pattern was explored, until the remaining factors were unable to fully explain the data. Results from and details of this analysis can be found in Appendix B.

APPENDIX B

# Details of Qualitative Comparative Analysis

The QCA approach we employed is designed to reduce patterns of observed factors to the minimum set sufficient to explain the outcomes (that is what prime implicants *are*). Because of the co-occurrence of so many positive factors in all the COIN wins and their rarity in COIN losses, we (and QCA) were unable to make any discrimination between a double handful of equally plausible sets of prime implicants.[1] To give a simple example: If *A* and *B* both occur in every win and never in a loss, which is more important, *A* or *B*? Discrimination is impossible.

In our QCA, we entered the factor stacks for the 12 approaches to COIN for which we found strong support at the bivariate level into fsQCA:[2]

---

[1] Conceivably, if we had more cases, we (and QCA) would be better able to discriminate. The addition of even a few cases that were COIN wins but had fewer of the positive COIN practices or that were COIN losses but had more of the positive COIN practices would help eliminate some of the good practices from being possible prime implicants and perhaps allow us to at least identify tiers of good practices, with the top tier being most important or essential and a second tier being beneficial but less critical. Of course, if in a larger set of data a single case drives the outcome of the analysis, we should rightly be concerned with the possibility of a truly exceptional narrative or Type I error.

[2] The bivariate analysis found strong support for 13 approaches. One of them, continuation and contestation, is an insurgent approach rather than a COIN approach. For this reason we exclude it from the QCA. As indicated in Appendix A, fsQCA would only resolve truth tables based on 11 factors at a time. While we could not test all 12 approaches at once, we were very quickly able to remove "At least three tangible support reduction factors present?" as it is the only factor in all of the data that constitutes a prime implicant all by itself (see Table B.2). After removing that candidate, we rotated the other approaches' factor stacks

1. both development factors
2. at least one pacification factor
3. at least two government legitimacy factors
4. at least two cost-benefit factors
5. flow of cross-border insurgent support decreased or was absent
6. at least two strategic communication factors
7. at least three COIN FM factors
8. at least two "beat-cop" factors
9. at least two "boots on the ground" factors
10. at least three tangible support factors reduced
11. at least one intelligence factor
12. flexibility and adaptability.

Table B.1 displays the truth table for these 12 factor stacks and whether the case was a COIN win. Remember, as in all of our data, 1 corresponds to the presence of a factor, 0 its absence. Each row in Table B.1 represents a pattern of factor presence and absence that appears in the observed data. Remember that all possible patterns of 12 binary independent variables plus the outcome would be $2^{12}$ rows; patterns that did not occur in the data were omitted. Patterns that occurred repeatedly are so indicated in the column "Number of Cases for Row." So, for example, the very first row of data in the table describes the pattern of factors present in three of the 30 cases; the last row of data in the table describes 10 cases. Eighteen distinct patterns of these 12 factors plus the outcome occur in the 30 cases.

Table B.1 includes several pieces of summary information. The right margin shows the sum of COIN approach factor stacks present for that row. For example, the first row of data (which we have already established as representing three cases) includes all 12 of the strongly supported approaches' factor stacks. The lower margin includes two summary numbers, the number of times each factor stack appears in a winning case and the number of times each factor stack appears in a losing case. So, for example, looking at the bottom margin for the first

in and out of the analysis, finally removing a factor once it had had a chance to join a set of prime implicants with all of the factors being tested.

**Table B.1**
**Truth Table for 12 Strongly Supported Approaches to COIN and Case Outcome**

| Both Development Factors | 1+ Pacification Factor | 2+ Government Legitimacy Factors | 2+ Cost-Benefit Factors | Reduced Cross-Border Insurgent Support | 2+ Strategic Communication Factors | 3+ COIN FM Factors | 2+ "Beat-Cop" Factors | 2+ "Boots on the Ground" Factors | 3+ Tangible Support Factors Reduced | 1+ Intelligence Factor | Flexibility and Adaptability | COIN Win | Number of Cases for Row | Sum of Approaches in Row |
|---|---|---|---|---|---|---|---|---|---|---|---|---|---|---|
| 1 | 1 | 1 | 1 | 1 | 1 | 1 | 1 | 1 | 1 | 1 | 1 | 1 | 3 | **12** |
| 0 | 1 | 1 | 1 | 1 | 1 | 1 | 1 | 1 | 1 | 1 | 1 | 1 | 1 | **11** |
| 1 | 1 | 1 | 0 | 1 | 1 | 1 | 1 | 1 | 1 | 0 | 1 | 1 | 1 | **10** |
| 0 | 1 | 1 | 0 | 1 | 1 | 1 | 1 | 1 | 1 | 0 | 1 | 1 | 1 | **9** |
| 0 | 1 | 1 | 0 | 1 | 1 | 1 | 1 | 0 | 1 | 1 | 1 | 1 | 1 | **9** |
| 0 | 1 | 0 | 1 | 1 | 1 | 0 | 1 | 0 | 1 | 1 | 1 | 1 | 1 | **8** |
| 0 | 0 | 1 | 0 | 0 | 0 | 0 | 0 | 0 | 0 | 0 | 0 | 0 | 1 | **1** |
| 0 | 0 | 1 | 0 | 0 | 0 | 0 | 0 | 0 | 0 | 0 | 1 | 0 | 1 | **2** |
| 0 | 0 | 0 | 0 | 0 | 0 | 0 | 1 | 0 | 0 | 0 | 0 | 0 | 1 | **1** |
| 0 | 0 | 1 | 0 | 0 | 0 | 0 | 1 | 0 | 0 | 0 | 0 | 0 | 1 | **2** |
| 0 | 0 | 0 | 0 | 0 | 0 | 1 | 1 | 0 | 0 | 0 | 1 | 0 | 1 | **3** |
| 0 | 0 | 0 | 0 | 0 | 1 | 0 | 0 | 0 | 0 | 0 | 0 | 0 | 1 | **1** |
| 0 | 1 | 0 | 0 | 0 | 1 | 0 | 1 | 0 | 0 | 0 | 0 | 0 | 1 | **3** |
| 0 | 0 | 0 | 0 | 1 | 0 | 0 | 0 | 0 | 0 | 0 | 1 | 0 | 1 | **2** |
| 0 | 0 | 0 | 0 | 0 | 0 | 0 | 0 | 1 | 0 | 0 | 1 | 0 | 1 | **2** |
| 0 | 0 | 0 | 0 | 0 | 0 | 0 | 0 | 1 | 0 | 0 | 0 | 0 | 1 | **1** |
| 0 | 0 | 0 | 0 | 0 | 0 | 0 | 0 | 0 | 0 | 0 | 1 | 0 | 2 | **1** |
| 0 | 0 | 0 | 0 | 0 | 0 | 0 | 0 | 0 | 0 | 0 | 0 | 0 | 10 | **0** |
| **4** | **8** | **7** | **5** | **8** | **8** | **7** | **8** | **6** | **8** | **6** | **8** | = no. of times realized in a win | | |
| **0** | **1** | **2** | **0** | **1** | **2** | **1** | **4** | **2** | **0** | **0** | **6** | = no. of times realized in a loss | | |

column, we see that both development factors are present in four winning cases and no losing cases. These numbers take into account the fact that some rows in the table represent multiple cases. The summaries in the bottom margins simply repeat what was already presented in the bivariate analysis of each approach.

A close examination of Table B.1 reveals many things. The first five rows of the table cover all eight COIN-winning cases; all lower rows are case losses. Looking at the right margin, we see that three cases realized all 12 factor stacks for the strongly supported approaches (Peru, Senegal, and Sierra Leone) and that all winning cases realized at least eight of the 12. This confirms what we already knew: Good COIN practices run in packs. It is similarly striking to examine the last row of data in the table and see that 10 cases (the last row represents 10 full cases) had absolutely none of the strongly supported approaches' factor stacks—and, of course, all were losses.

This 18-row truth table is what we input into fsQCA. The software uses Boolean algebra to summarize the truth table with minimally sufficient patterns of factors called prime implicants. Ideally, we would be able to mathematically produce only a small number of prime implicants, and the approaches whose factor stacks composed those prime implicants would receive stronger support still. Unfortunately, the fact that so many of the factor stacks are consistently present in the winning cases means that many different Boolean reductions into prime implicants are possible.

As described in Appendix A, factors that were found to be part of prime implicant groups were cycled in and out and ultimately removed so that all factors had an opportunity to interact with all the others and join prime implicant patterns. Following this process produced 16 separate and equally plausible sets of prime implicants.

Each of the prime implicant groups shown in Table B.2 is equally plausible. That is, each fully explains the data (perfectly discriminates between a COIN win and a COIN loss for all cases), and there is no strong theoretical reason to accept one over the other. The only possible justification for a preference would be Occam's razor, which gives preference to simple explanations over complex ones. This would appear to slightly prejudice prime implicant groups containing only

**Table B.2**
**Prime Implicants for 12 Strongly Supported Approaches and Case Outcome**

| Prime Implicant Group | Description |
|---|---|
| One prime implicant | |
| 1 | At least 3 tangible support factors reduced |
| 2 | At least 2 strategic communication factors × flow of cross-border insurgent support decreased or absent |
| 3 | At least 2 strategic communication factors × flexibility and adaptability |
| 4 | At least 1 pacification factor × flexibility and adaptability |
| 5 | At least 1 pacification factor × flow of cross-border insurgent support decreased or absent |
| 6 | At least 2 "beat-cop" factors × flow of cross-border insurgent support decreased or absent |
| Two prime implicants | |
| 7 | At least 1 intelligence factor *and* at least 2 strategic communication factors × at least 3 COIN FM factors |
| 8 | At least 1 intelligence factor *and* at least 2 strategic communication factors × at least 2 government legitimacy factors |
| 9 | At least 1 intelligence factor *and* at least 3 COIN FM factors × at least 1 pacification factor |
| 10 | At least 1 intelligence factor *and* at least 3 COIN FM factors × at least 2 government legitimacy factors |
| 11 | At least 1 intelligence factor *and* at least 1 pacification factor × at least 2 government legitimacy factors |
| 12 | At least 2 cost-benefit factors *and* at least 2 strategic communication factors × at least 3 COIN FM factors |
| 13 | At least 2 cost-benefit factors *and* at least 2 strategic communication factors × at least 2 government legitimacy factors |
| 14 | At least 2 cost-benefit factors *and* at least 1 pacification factor × at least 2 government legitimacy factors |
| 15 | At least 2 cost-benefit factors *and* at least 3 COIN FM factors × at least 1 pacification factor |
| 16 | At least 2 cost-benefit factors *and* at least 3 COIN FM factors × at least 2 government legitimacy factors |

one prime implicant. However, none of the groups requires more than two prime implicants, and none of them requires more than three factor stacks to compose its implicants—slim purchase for Occam.[3]

So, for example, prime implicant group 2 consists of "at least 2 strategic communication factors × flow of cross-border insurgent support decreased or absent." When multiplying binary variables, if either is absent, the product goes to 0 ($1 \times 0 = 0$, $0 \times 1 = 0$, and $0 \times 0 = 0$). Only when both factors are present is the resulting product a 1, indicating presence of the combined factor (in this case, a prime implicant). So, cases having at least three strategic communication factors and a decreasing or absent flow of cross-border insurgent support are always COIN wins; those lacking one or both factors are always COIN losses. The contents of prime implicant group 2 are sufficient to perfectly discriminate all the cases into wins and losses (as are all of the other prime implicant groups).

For readers for whom this discussion is not intuitive, we provide an alternative presentation of some of the prime implicant groups in Table B.2 by way of example. See Figures B.1–B.4.

**Figure B.1**
**Flow Chart for Prime Implicant Group 1**

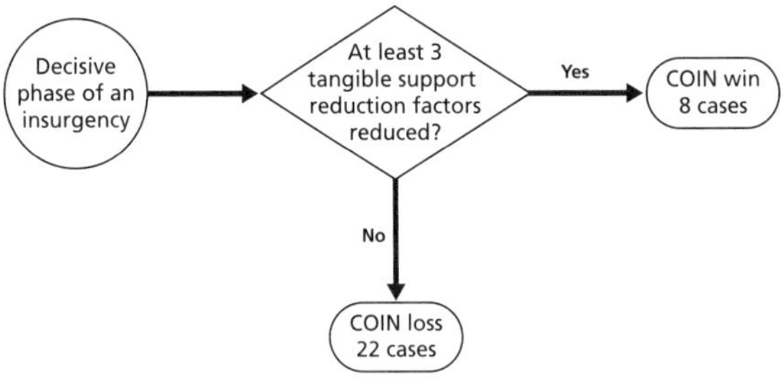


RAND *MG964-B.1*

[3] Regarding Occam's razor, see Encyclopædia Britannica Online, "Ockham's Razor," undated. The astute reader will notice that some of the flowcharts in Figures B.1–B.4 contain more than three factors; however, those with more than three contain one or more "or" operators such that the number of factors *required* to fully discriminate the outcome of all cases is never more than three; one simply has a choice regarding which three.

**Figure B.2**
**Flow Chart for Prime Implicant Group 3**

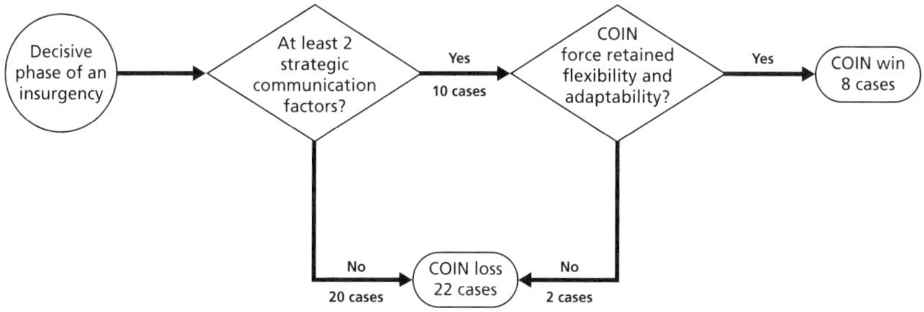


RAND *MG964-B.2*

**Figure B.3**
**Flow Chart for Prime Implicant Group 5**

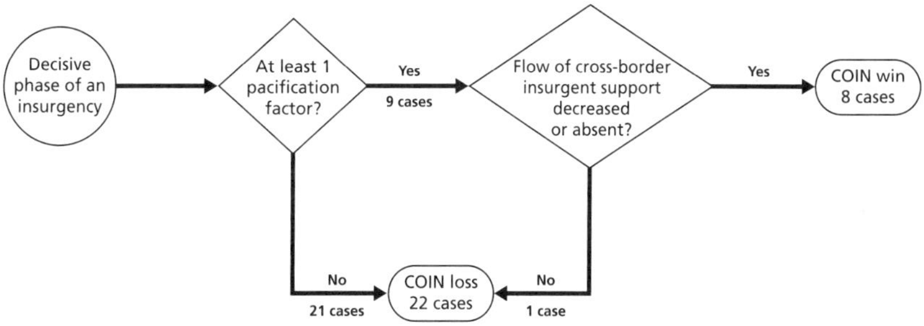


RAND *MG964-B.3*

Each of the prime implicant group figures follows flowcharting rules and the same logic. Each begins with the same start condition, "decisive phase of an insurgency." From there, each proceeds through one or more decision diamonds, with patterns of presence or absence of factor stacks (yes or no) ultimately discriminating cases into COIN wins or COIN losses. As noted, each set of prime implicants completely describes the outcomes of the cases.

Where an "or" is present in one of the flowcharts, it indicates that all of the outcomes in the data can be completely resolved using any of the factor paths subsequent to the "or." This actually implies more prime implicants than the number of figures. For example, see Figure B.4.

**Figure B.4**
**Flow Chart for Prime Implicant Groups 9 and 10**

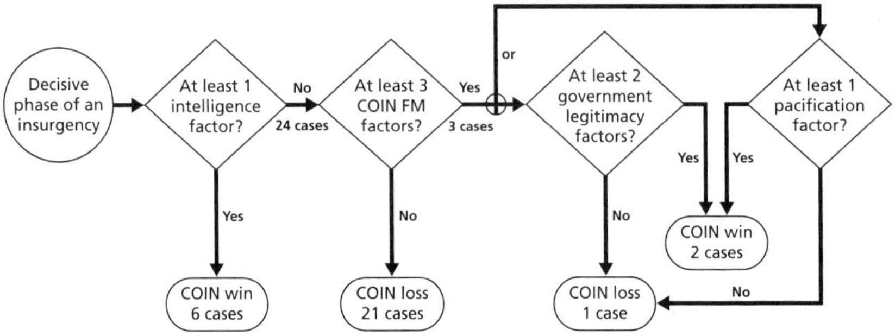


RAND *MG964-B.4*

By indicating that "at least 1 intelligence factor" plus "at least 3 COIN FM factors" and either at "least 2 government legitimacy factors" or "at least 1 pacification factor" is sufficient to explain the outcome of all cases, two sets of prime implicants are implied: group 9, intelligence *and* FM 3-24 × government legitimacy; and group 10, intelligence *and* FM 3-24 × democracy.

While each individual flowchart appears tantalizingly interesting, the fact that they are all equally plausible ruins that illusion. Any of a host of prime implicant groups can fully explain these data because so many factors associated with supported COIN approaches appear in so many of the COIN wins and so few of the COIN losses. Ultimately, the QCA just confirms what we had already concluded from the stacked bivariate analysis: Good COIN practices run in packs.

The QCA approach was worthwhile, however, because, in addition to confirming the bivariate analysis, it dismisses the possibility of multivariate interactions camouflaging exceptions to our bivariate conclusions. For example, factor stacks for all approaches, save tangible support reduction, fail to perfectly predict the data; they either do not occur in at least one win or do occur in at least one loss. Were it always the same wins or same losses (some truly exceptional case or cases) that all of these factor stacks were not predicting, we would not see that strictly from the bivariate analysis. Both QCA and the good versus bad factor summation preclude the possibility of such an exceptional case. Many different patterns of prime implicants fully explain the data, as does the summed contrast of good COIN practices versus bad ones.

APPENDIX C

# Possible Criticisms of the Analyses and Response Commentary

During quality assurance review and when presenting preliminary findings in forums arranged by our sponsor, we had several opportunities to receive feedback and criticism of our analyses. Most of these criticisms have been addressed and wholly resolved as part of our revisions. Some, however, are either irresolvable or are not really problems. We list several of these open criticisms here to demonstrate our awareness of these concerns and to offer commentary on the extent to which our analysis is vulnerable to any specific criticism.

## Case Selection

Any set or sample of historical cases is open to criticism. Do the selected cases go back far enough in history? Do they go too far? Are the cases representative of the population? What are the implications of excluding unresolved cases? What about coups and insurrections? Of the various questions and criticisms, possible and offered, of the set of cases we selected, three merit discussion.

### Few Occupations

First, the 30 most recent resolved insurgencies include an unfortunately small number of cases in which the principal COIN actor is an external force (three of the 30 cases). This is unfortunate because three cases is too few to discriminate whether COIN involving external actors is significantly different from COIN without. Because U.S. engagement in COIN will always be as an external force (unless one imagines insurgency in the United States as a future possibility), and because our primary audience is the U.S. defense community, we would like to be able to speak with authority regarding this subclass of COIN. These data do not allow us to do so. Were we to choose additional cases to examine using the methods we use here, we would endeavor to include more external-actor COIN operations.

### Short Cases

Second, one reviewer noted that our population of cases tends toward shorter insurgencies than the superpopulation of all 20th- and 21st-century insurgencies. This observation is correct. The average duration of all the resolved insurgencies in Libicki's insurgency list, from which we selected our cases, is 12.26 years; our 30 cases have an average duration of 8.17 years. The prime driver for this difference is a handful of very lengthy insurgencies beginning in the 20th century (the insurgency in Burma that lasted from 1948 to 2006, the 1960–1996 Guatemalan insurgency, and the South African insurgency from 1960 to 1994, for example). There are unresolved insurgencies that began after 1978 that would have been part of our data if they were finished. Some of these insurgencies promise to be just as long as those begun earlier in the century (e.g., the India-Naxalite insurgency is already 29 years old, Uganda's struggle with the Lord's Resistance Army has been ongoing for 22 years). Excluding unresolved cases has the same effect as excluding (some) very long cases. To the extent that extremely long insurgencies differ from short or modestly long insurgencies, those differences are not captured in our analyses.

### Resurgent Insurgencies

A third concern is that we consider some of our cases resolved when insurgent conflict has subsequently resumed. The selection criteria that Libicki used to identify the chronological bounds of a given insurgency were based on the annual casualty threshold falling below a certain level. This could (and does) cause us to treat cases as having ended when in fact the insurgents have merely withdrawn to havens and are licking their wounds, marshaling their strength, revisiting their strategies, or otherwise preparing to continue their insurgency at a (much) later date. One example of this is the PKK in Turkey, an insurgency that we treat as having ended in 1999; renewed conflict in the area persists as of this writing.

How to discern the real "end" of an insurgency is problematic, given the concern noted in the previous paragraph or the propensity of negotiated settlements to result in a small splinter of residual insurgents who continue to engage in resistance activities—but usually at a level that constitutes no real threat to the state. When is a subsequent outbreak of conflict a new insurgency or just a continuation of the previous one? Barring research into exactly that issue, we believe that a minimum casualty threshold is a good metric. What is the difference between the residual splinter of a defeated insurgency that can be dealt with strictly as a law-enforcement problem and a dormant insurgency? We do not know, but we maintain that either outcome is better for the state than an active insurgency.

## Data Imprecision

None of the authors is particularly expert in most of the insurgencies included in the case studies. All are experienced in historical case-study research, and data for each case were drawn from a variety of sources. That said, given the scope of the data (76 factors and between two and five phases per case), some of the present/absent judgments made in establishing the data matrix to support our quantitative analyses are probably wrong. While we accept that a certain number of errors are possible (even likely), we take solace in the fact that our core findings are so robust that they are invulnerable to whatever small errors exist in the data.

Several commentators have asked whether we used multiple analysts for each assessment to ensure consistent interpretation of factors. The use of multiple assessors of the same data (even if just to test the data) is an important part of what is usually called testing or establishing intercoder reliability. While intercoder reliability confirmation is a common approach in content analysis or other analysis in which there is a fixed (and relatively small) amount of data for each case or item, such a formal exercise was wholly impractical for this research. The sheer volume of the information that an analyst needed to review to complete a case study rendered it fiscally infeasible to have duplication of effort in this area. We did, however, hold regular team meetings to discuss the factors, their interpretations, and their assessment, usually in the context of actual cases with real examples. See the discussion in Appendix A for details of our assessment process.

## Binary Scoring in a Complex World

All of the factors in our quantitative analysis are binary: present/absent, 1/0. This has pros and cons. On the plus side, it makes assessment easier (an analyst just needs to make a threshold adjudication) and some forms of analysis tractable. It also protects us from false precision. On the downside, sometimes the reality is more complicated than "present or absent." Sometimes, the correct assessment of a factor is "yes, but." *Yes*, the factor threshold or criteria for assessing this factor as present have been met, *but* there is more to it in this particular case. Throughout our data collection, we were careful to note "yes, but" situations for several reasons. First, we raised them in team meetings to see whether a "yes, but" assessment was unique to a single case or something that characterized several cases. If it was unique to a specific case, then it might be an important part of that case's narrative. If "yes, but" occurred for the same factor across various cases, we took that as an invitation to revise the wording of the factor or to change the factor's threshold. These changes helped the analysts ensure that the factor as scored in their cases accurately reflected both the approach or tenet and the real details of the case.

Another downside to binary scoring is that present or absent assessment deprives us of the ability to assess the impact of more or less of something. Engendering a perception of security is good. Is engendering *more* of a perception of security *more* good? Binary assessment precludes us from trying to answer that question. The factor stacks we use to assess the various approaches provide some incremental assessment. Do better results accrue to those who follow more than a bare minimum of the tenets of a given approach? There, we can see whether cases in which more of the factors for an approach are present are even more likely to be wins.

### "Mixed" Outcomes

Particularly concerning in our binary-only assessment were mixed outcomes. First, note that while we scored a "mixed outcome" as present or absent for each phase of each case, we did not end up using it in any of our analyses. This was partially because "mixed" is problematic, and partially because it ended up providing no traction in the preliminary analyses.

"Mixed" as an outcome is problematic in part because it is very difficult to consistently identify a threshold. Insurgency outcomes are a study in shades of gray. One would be perfectly justified in assessing almost all insurgency outcomes as "mixed." Very rarely does the prevailing side get everything it wanted. Compromise and settlement of some sort are frequent, as are amnesties, concessions, and reforms. Fortunately, for every case and phase, we were clearly able to ascertain which side had the better of the outcome and whether it was a little bit mixed, a lot mixed, or hardly mixed at all.

### Assumption of Equal Weight

Table 4.1 in Chapter Four makes an implicit assumption of equal weight of factors. That is, adding up factors assumes that they are all equal and subject to addition rules. Two good factors is twice as good as one good factor. *While that particular analysis implies equal weight of factors, we do not believe or wish to make that assumption more generally.* The 1s and 0s representing present and absent are not intended to be added up. These factors are not of uniform importance; some are much more important than others. In fact, had fewer of them occurred together, our QCA might have allowed us to say *which* are more important than others. However, many positive factors do occur together with great frequency in cases in which the COIN force prevailed, and vice versa for COIN losses. This prevents us from getting maximum mileage out of our QCA but in itself constitutes a very interesting finding. Showing the sum of good practices minus the sum of bad practices is just a striking way to illustrate that point. We do not intend for readers to make anything of the individual scores themselves—just the fact that there is a gap of indeterminate size between the practice makeup of winning COIN forces and losing COIN forces.

All of our factor stacks also implicitly assume that factors are of equal weight. This is a more robust assumption, not because we believe the weights are equal but because of the empirical cut points. A factor stack that has "at least 2 [approach] factors" works because an empirical pattern emerges for all cases with at least two factors in that factor stack. Though the language of the factor stack implies equal weight of the combined factors, we do not maintain that assumption through our findings and recommendations. That is, we do not then recommend that those seeking success in COIN incorporate at least two of a supported approach's factors but that those seeking success at COIN employ all the tenets of that supported approach (and as many other successful approaches as possible, since victory has a thousand fathers!).

### Factor Stack Empirical Cut Points and COIN Approaches

Our decision to let the data speak and identify thresholds for satisfaction criteria for the adherence to certain approaches based on empirically observed cut points (see the discussion in Chapter Four) is open to criticism. One might argue that we should have set a theoretically based standard, either across all approaches (e.g., a threshold of 50 percent or even of 100 percent of an approach's factors must be present to qualify) or based on individual approaches (e.g., How many of these factors or practices do the proponents of an approach suggest are necessary in order to prevail?).

Our decision to use empirically observed cut points is not a conservative one; it shows each approach in its best possible light by maximizing the ability of the factors to predict COIN success versus failure. We do not present the sums of factors for each approach, though they were part of our preliminary analysis. In our defense, for all approaches receiving strong support in our analysis (as listed in Table 3.23 in Chapter Three), choosing a higher threshold would only increase the predictive power of the single-factor expression of the theory and the outcome. That is, for each supported approach, higher thresholds would exclude case losses, ultimately to the point of perfection. Consider, for example, Table C.1.

Imagine if we had used a higher threshold. For the sake of argument, suppose we had insisted on the presence of 50 percent of a theory's factors before considering the theory to be implemented. Standard rounding practice for 50 percent of seven factors would require that at least four factors be present. If we used that threshold, then we would conclude that strategic communication was properly implemented in only four of the 30 cases. However, we would conclude that it perfectly predicts a win every time it is employed. Similar patterns would be observed for all of the supported approaches: Fewer cases would get credit for implementing each approach, but each approach would be shown to be even more successful as a predictor of outcome.

**Qualitative Comparative Analysis with Higher Thresholds for the Approaches.** The thresholds to receive credit for implementing an approach also have implications for the QCA. A reviewer expert in QCA pointed out that by using relatively low thresholds for conformity to the different approaches (i.e., requiring only one or two of a handful of

**Table C.1**
**Sum of Strategic Communication Factors Versus Case Outcome (empirical cut point in red)**

| Sum of strategic communication factors | Case Outcome: COIN Loss | Case Outcome: COIN Win |
|---|---|---|
| 7 | 0 | 1 |
| 6 | 0 | 2 |
| 5 | 0 | 1 |
| 4 | 0 | 0 |
| 3 | 1 | 4 |
| 2 | 1 | 4 |
| 1 | 5 | 0 |
| 0 | 15 | 0 |

factors to count as having implemented an approach), we increased the likelihood that more cases would conform and thus the likelihood that we would be unable to distinguish differences between cases. This is one possible explanation for the failure of QCA to better discriminate between the different approaches.

To test the validity of this concern, we ran an additional round of QCA after increasing the thresholds required for a case to count as having implemented any of the 12 strongly supported approaches. The new thresholds were set either so that all cases having that value were COIN wins or at the highest observed value for that factor (only when at least one loss had the highest observed value). This resulted in no change in threshold for five of the 12 factors. Table C.2 presents the changes to scoring for each approach.

These new higher thresholds were used to score the presence or absence of 12 strongly supporting factors for each case. Table C.3 is the truth table for the revised high-threshold scoring. Like Table B.1 in Appendix B, this truth table summarizes all combinations of these

**Table C.2**
**Changes to Factor Stack Thresholds for Additional QCA**

| Approach | Original Threshold | New Threshold |
|---|---|---|
| Development | Both factors | Both factors (unchanged) |
| Pacification | 1 or more of 3 factors | 2 or more of 3 factors |
| Government legitimacy | 2 or more of 5 factors | All 5 |
| Cost-benefit | 2 or more of 5 factors | All 5 |
| Border control | Factor present | Factor present (unchanged) |
| Strategic communication | 2 or more of 7 factors | 5 or more of 7 factors |
| COIN FM | 3 or more of 9 factors | 4 or more of 9 factors |
| "Beat cop" | 2 or more of 4 factors | All 4 |
| "Boots on the ground" | 2 or more of 3 factors | All 3 |
| Tangible support reduction | 3 or more of 10 factors | 3 or more of 10 factors (unchanged) |
| Intelligence | 1 of 2 factors | 1 of 2 factors (unchanged) |
| Flexibility and adaptability | Factor present | Factor present (unchanged) |

**Table C.3**
**Truth Table for 12 Strongly Supported Approaches to COIN and Case Outcome, with Higher Thresholds**

| Both Development Factors | 2+ (of 3) Pacification Factors | All 5 Government Legitimacy Factors | All 5 Cost-Benefit Factors | Reduced Cross-Border Insurgent Support | 5+ (of 7) Strategic Communication Factors | 4+ (of 9) COIN FM Factors | All 4 "Beat-Cop" Factors | All 3 "Boots on the Ground" Factors | 3+ (of 10) Tangible Support Factors Reduced | 1+ (of 2) Intelligence Factors | Flexibility and Adaptability | COIN Win | Number of Cases for Row | Sum of Approaches in Row | Case |
|---|---|---|---|---|---|---|---|---|---|---|---|---|---|---|---|
| 1 | 1 | 1 | 1 | 1 | 1 | 1 | 1 | 1 | 1 | 1 | 1 | 1 | 1 | **12** | Senegal |
| 1 | 1 | 1 | 0 | 1 | 1 | 1 | 1 | 0 | 1 | 1 | 1 | 1 | 1 | **10** | Peru |
| 1 | 1 | 0 | 1 | 1 | 1 | 1 | 1 | 0 | 1 | 1 | 1 | 1 | 1 | **10** | Sierra Leone |
| 1 | 1 | 1 | 0 | 1 | 1 | 1 | 1 | 0 | 1 | 0 | 1 | 1 | 1 | **9** | El Salvador |
| 0 | 1 | 0 | 1 | 1 | 0 | 1 | 0 | 0 | 1 | 1 | 1 | 1 | 1 | **7** | Turkey |
| 0 | 0 | 0 | 0 | 1 | 0 | 1 | 1 | 1 | 1 | 0 | 1 | 1 | 1 | **6** | Uganda |
| 0 | 0 | 0 | 1 | 1 | 0 | 0 | 0 | 0 | 1 | 1 | 1 | 1 | 1 | **5** | Croatia |
| 0 | 0 | 0 | 0 | 1 | 0 | 0 | 0 | 0 | 1 | 1 | 1 | 1 | 1 | **4** | Algeria |
| 0 | 0 | 0 | 0 | 1 | 0 | 0 | 0 | 0 | 0 | 0 | 1 | 0 | 1 | **2** | |
| 0 | 0 | 0 | 0 | 0 | 0 | 0 | 0 | 0 | 0 | 0 | 1 | 0 | 5 | **1** | |
| 0 | 0 | 0 | 0 | 0 | 0 | 0 | 0 | 0 | 0 | 0 | 0 | 0 | 16 | **0** | |
| **4** | **5** | **3** | **4** | **8** | **4** | **6** | **5** | **2** | **8** | **6** | **8** | = no. of times realized in a win | | | |
| **0** | **0** | **0** | **0** | **1** | **0** | **0** | **0** | **0** | **0** | **0** | **6** | = no. of times realized in a loss | | | |

12 revised-threshold approaches and the outcomes that appear in the data.

Several observations about Table C.3 are noteworthy. First, each of the top eight rows in the table represents only a single case; this means that none of the COIN wins has the exact same pattern of high-threshold approaches present. Second, good COIN practices continue to run in packs; while only one case still has all 12 approaches applied under the higher thresholds, fully half (four) of the cases have at least nine high-threshold approaches in play. Every winning case has at least four approaches in play. It is further striking how few approaches are in play in the COIN losses. The last row of Table C.3 shows that fully 16 losing COIN forces implemented none of the high-threshold approaches, five losing COIN forces implemented a single high-threshold approach, and a single losing COIN force implemented a single approach.

Performing QCA on this reduced set does produce fewer prime implicants, but it still does not allow us to discriminate a very small number of most important COIN practices. Table C.4 lists the prime implicants produced by this set of iterations of QCA.

As before, tangible support reduction remains the only approach to perfectly predict wins and losses. While the three remaining prime implicant sets seem to favor intelligence as a critical factor, we caution the reader to not make too much of this.

The high thresholds used here are probably too high in several cases, discounting cases in which an approach was actually (or mostly)

**Table C.4**
**Prime Implicants for 12 Strongly Supported Approaches and Case Outcome, with Higher Thresholds**

| Prime Implicant Group | Description |
|---|---|
| One prime implicant | |
| 1 | 3+ (of 10) tangible support factors reduced |
| Two prime implicants | |
| 2 | 1+ (of 2) intelligence factors *and* 4+ (of 9) COIN FM factors |
| 3 | 1+ (of 2) intelligence factors *and* all 4 "beat-cop" factors |
| Three prime implicants | |
| 4 | 1+ (of 2) intelligence factors *and* all 3 "boots on the ground" factors *and* one of the following: both development factors *or* 2+ (of 3) pacification factors *or* all 5 government legitimacy factors *or* 5+ (of 7) strategic communication factors |

implemented. Further, intelligence, which appears prominently in this new set of prime implicants, had a rather low "high threshold": having at least one of the two intelligence factors. Having at least one of the two intelligence factors occurs in six of the eight COIN wins and in none of the losses. Having both intelligence factors occurs in only four cases. If that were the threshold (and why not? this is "high-threshold" analysis, and several other approaches end up requiring every factor present in the high-threshold version), it would not show as well.

Further, a close consideration of Table C.4 jointly with Table C.3 reveals that the results are driven primarily by two cases. Algeria, which contains only four of the 12 high-threshold approaches, severely constrains the number of approaches that can contribute to prime implicants. Similarly, the COIN loss represented in row 9 in Table C.3 (which happens to be Burundi) impugns an approach that would otherwise make a good showing: border control. Further compounding this, border control is one of the four high-threshold approaches in play in Algeria, leaving tangible support reduction (which we already know is a strong implicant), border control (damaged as a predictor by its presence in the loss in Burundi), flexibility and adaptability (which appears in all COIN wins but in six losses, too), and intelligence. This, then, is why the QCA for the high-threshold approaches produces the results it does. If one is willing to assign more importance to the Algerian COIN case than it perhaps deserves, then one might believe that tangible support reduction and actionable intelligence are the most important of the collected approaches to COIN. However, the more robust finding is that they are just two among a host of mutually supporting and effective approaches to COIN because good COIN practices run in packs.

As a final note, the full data for each case are presented in the accompanying volume, *Victory Has a Thousand Fathers: Detailed Counterinsurgency Case Studies*.[1] Those curious about the analytical implication of different thresholds or cut points for the satisfaction of an approach are welcome to experiment with the data.

---

[1] Paul, Clarke, and Grill, 2010.

## Tautological Relationships Between Factors and Outcomes

In the discussion of the effectiveness of amnesty as a COIN approach (see Chapter Three), we note that we cannot test amnesty as an approach to COIN because we cannot disentangle the causal order of amnesty and resolution of insurgency. This concern might apply to some other factors to make some of our arguments appear tautological: You win because you are winning. Which factors are themselves steps on the path to victory, and which are just symptoms of COIN success?

There are certainly factors in this analysis that are potentially vulnerable to this criticism. The oft-repeated aphorism that "correlation is not causation" is certainly true. Fortunately, we do not make any strong causal arguments, in part because so many good COIN practices occur together that we cannot arbitrate between their many possible causal contributions. If "doing all the things that winners do will make you win" is a tautology, so be it; it proves true in all the cases in this analysis and has clear implications for forces and governments that are serious about COIN.[2]

## The Way Ahead

The data collected for this research are extremely rich and will support further analysis. Though they are spread throughout the individual case histories, we report the data in full in the accompanying volume.

---

[2] A reviewer raised the concern that this logic, taken out of context, has serious flaws. For example, one could glibly say that "driving a Mercedes must mean you are successful because successful people drive Mercedes" and then turn that kind of criticism back on this analysis. In our defense, we note that all of the approaches employed in this analysis provide good underlying logical and theoretical reasons for one to believe that they could have a causal connection with the outcome of an insurgency (except amnesty, as noted above). While our analysis does not allow us to tease out which approaches contribute the most causal heft, we have very good reason to believe that some combination of the positive factors related to these approaches really is causing the observed outcomes.

Inasmuch as further interesting questions about COIN can be answered with these data, our analyses also raise some questions that cannot be answered with the data. For example,

- What determines the duration of an insurgency, either in phases or in actual time?
- What, if anything, changes when the primary COIN force is an external force?

Only three of the 30 most recent resolved insurgencies were opposed primarily by an external force (all were COIN losses), yet the United States will always be an external actor when engaged in or assisting with COIN.

- What causes recurrence or relapse?

Several of our cases occur in the same country (Afghanistan three times, Nicaragua twice, Zaire/DRC twice), and other cases have seen new flare-ups after their resolution (the PKK in Turkey, as a single example).

All of these topics remain ripe for investigation using methods similar to those employed here.

# References


Abbott, Andrew, "Conceptions of Time and Events in Social Science Methods: Causal and Narrative Approaches," *Historical Methods*, Vol. 23, No. 4, 1990, pp. 140–150.

Aminzade, Ronald, "Historical Sociology and Time," *Sociological Methods and Research*, Vol. 20, No. 4, 1992, pp. 456–480.

Anders, David P., *Developing an Operational Level Strategic Communication Model for Counterinsurgency*, Carlisle, Pa.: U.S. Army War College, 2009.

Ball, Nicole, and Luc van de Goor, *Disarmament, Demobilization and Reintegration: Mapping Issues, Dilemmas and Guiding Principles*, Clingendael, Netherlands: Netherlands Institute of International Relations, August 2006.

Boole, George, *An Investigation of the Laws of Thought*, Amherst, N.Y.: Prometheus, 2003.

Clancy, James, and Chuck Crosset, "Measuring Effectiveness in Irregular Warfare," *Parameters*, Summer 2007, pp. 88–100.

Cohen, Eliot, Conrad Crane, Jan Horvath, and John Nagl, "Principles, Imperatives, and Paradoxes of Counterinsurgency," *Military Review*, March–April 2006, pp. 49–53.

Corum, James S., *Training Indigenous Forces in Counterinsurgency: A Tale of Two Insurgencies*, Carlisle, Pa.: Strategic Studies Institute, U.S. Army War College, March 2006.

DeBray, Regis, *Revolution in the Revolution*, New York: Grove Press, 1967.

Edelstein, David, "Occupational Hazards: Why Military Occupations Succeed or Fail," *International Security*, Vol. 29, No. 1, Summer 2004, pp. 79–91.

Eder, Mari K., "Toward Strategic Communication," *Military Review*, July–August 2007, pp. 61–70.

Encyclopædia Britannica Online, "Ockham's Razor," undated. As of October 8, 2009:
http://www.britannica.com/EBchecked/topic/424706/Ockhams-razor

Faye, Wagane, *The Casamance Separatism: From Independence Claim to Resource Logic*, thesis, Monterey, Calif.: Naval Postgraduate School, June 2006.

Fearon, James D., and David D. Laitin, "Ethnicity, Insurgency, and Civil War," *American Political Science Review*, Vol. 97, No. 1, February 2003, pp. 75–90.

Felter, Joe, "Taking Guns to a Knife Fight: An Empirical Study of Effective Counterinsurgency," paper presented at the annual meeting of the American Political Science Association, Philadelphia, Pa., August 31, 2006. As of May 24, 2009:
http://www.allacademic.com/meta/p151510_index.html

Giampietri, Sergio M., and John H. Stone, Sr., *A Counterinsurgency Study: An Analysis of Local Defenses*, Monterey, Calif.: Naval Postgraduate School, September 2004.

Gompert, David C., John Gordon IV, Adam Grissom, David R. Frelinger, Seth G. Jones, Martin C. Libicki, Edward O'Connell, Brooke Stearns Lawson, and Robert E. Hunter, *War by Other Means—Building Complete and Balanced Capabilities for Counterinsurgency: RAND Counterinsurgency Study—Final Report*, Santa Monica, Calif.: RAND Corporation, MG-595/2-OSD, 2008. As of March 2, 2010:
http://www.rand.org/pubs/monographs/MG595.2/

Gray, Colin S., "Irregular Warfare: One Nature, Many Characters," *Strategic Studies Quarterly*, Winter 2007, pp. 35–57.

Greenhill, Kelly M., *Draining the Sea, or Feeding the Fire? The Use of Population Relocation in Counterinsurgency Operations*, Center for International Security and Cooperation, Stanford University, forthcoming.

Guevara, Ernesto "Che," *Guerrilla Warfare*, New York: Monthly Review Press, 1961.

Guillen, Abraham, *Philosophy of the Urban Guerrilla*, Donald C. Hodges, trans. and ed., New York: William Morrow, 1973.

Halloran, Richard, "Strategic Communication," *Parameters*, Autumn 2007, pp. 4–14.

Hammes, Thomas X., *The Sling and the Stone: On War in the 21st Century*, St. Paul, Minn.: Zenith Press, 2004.

———, "Why Study Small Wars?" *Small Wars Journal*, Vol. 1, April 2005, pp. 1–5.

Harrill, J. D., *Phased Insurgency Theory: Ramadi*, Quantico, Va.: U.S. Marine Corps Command and Staff College, 2008.

Headquarters, U.S. Department of the Army, and Headquarters, U.S. Marine Corps, *Counterinsurgency Field Manual*, Field Manual 3-24/Marine Corps Warfighting Publication 3-33.5, Chicago, Ill.: University of Chicago Press, 2007.

Hoffman, Frank G., "Neo-Classical Counterinsurgency?" *Parameters*, Summer 2007, pp. 71–87.

Humphreys, Macartan, and Jeremy M. Weinstein, "Demobilization and Reintegration," *Journal of Conflict Resolution*, Vol. 51, No. 4, 2007, pp. 531–567.

Huntington, Samuel, *Political Order in Changing Societies*, New Haven, Conn.: Yale University Press, 1968.

Joes, Anthony James, *Guerrilla Warfare: A Historical, Biographical, and Bibliographical Sourcebook*, Westport, Conn.: Greenwood Press, 1996.

Jones, Jeffrey B., "Strategic Communication: A Mandate for the United States," *Joint Force Quarterly*, No. 39, 4th Quarter 2005, pp. 108–114.

Josten, Richard J., "Strategic Communication: Key Enabler for Elements of National Power," *IO Sphere*, Summer 2006, pp. 16–20.

Kilcullen, David, "Twenty-Eight Articles: Fundamentals of Company-Level Counterinsurgency," *IO Sphere*, Summer 2006a, pp. 29–35.

———, "Three Pillars of Counterinsurgency," presentation, U.S. Government Counterinsurgency Conference, Washington, D.C., September 28, 2006b. As of November 4, 2008:
http://www.au.af.mil/au/awc/awcgate/uscoin/3pillars_of_counterinsurgency.pdf

Klare, Michael T., "The New Face of Combat: Terrorism and Irregular Warfare in the 21st Century," in Charles W. Kegley, Jr., ed., *The New Global Terrorism: Characteristics, Causes, Controls*, Upper Saddle River, N.J.: Prentice Hall, 2003, pp. 27–35.

Lawrence, T. E., "The Twenty-Seven Articles," *The Arab Bulletin*, August 20, 1917. As of November 3, 2009:
http://wwi.lib.byu.edu/index.php/The_27_Articles_of_T.E._Lawrence

Leites, Nathan Constantin, and Charles Wolf, Jr., *Rebellion and Authority: An Analytic Essay on Insurgent Conflicts*, Santa Monica, Calif.: RAND Corporation, R-462-ARPA, 1970. As of March 2, 2010:
http://www.rand.org/pubs/reports/R0462/

Libicki, Martin C., "Eighty-Nine Insurgencies: Outcomes and Endings," in David C. Gompert, John Gordon IV, Adam Grissom, David R. Frelinger, Seth G. Jones, Martin C. Libicki, Edward O'Connell, Brooke Stearns Lawson, and Robert E. Hunter, *War by Other Means—Building Complete and Balanced Capabilities for Counterinsurgency: RAND Counterinsurgency Study—Final Report*, Santa Monica, Calif.: RAND Corporation, MG-595/2-OSD, 2008, pp. 373–396. As of March 2, 2010:
http://www.rand.org/pubs/monographs/MG595.2/

Long, Austin, *On "Other War": Lessons from Five Decades of RAND Counterinsurgency Research*, Santa Monica, Calif.: RAND Corporation, MG-482-OSD, 2006. As of March 2, 2010: http://www.rand.org/pubs/monographs/MG482/

———, "The Anbar Awakening," *Survival*, Vol. 50, No. 2, April–May 2008, pp. 67–94.

Mao Tse-Tung, *On Protracted War*, Peking: People's Publishing House, 1954.

———, *On Guerrilla Warfare*, Samuel B. Griffith II, trans., New York: Praeger, 1961.

Marighella, Carlos, *Minimanual of the Urban Guerrilla*, 1969.

Markel, Wade, "Draining the Swamp: The British Strategy of Population Control," *Parameters*, Spring 2006, pp. 35–48.

Marks, Thomas A., *Insurgency in Nepal*, Carlisle, Pa.: Strategic Studies Institute, U.S. Army War College, December 2003.

McFate, Montgomery, and Andrea V. Jackson, "The Object Beyond War: Counterinsurgency and the Four Tools of Political Competition," *Military Review*, January–February 2006, pp. 13–26.

Metz, Steven, and Raymond Millen, *Insurgency and Counterinsurgency in the 21st Century: Reconceptualizing Threat and Response*, Carlisle, Pa.: Strategic Studies Institute, U.S. Army War College, November 2004.

Millen, Raymond A., *Afghanistan: Reconstituting a Collapsed State*, Carlisle, Pa.: Strategic Studies Institute, U.S. Army War College, April 2005.

Nagl, John, *Learning to Eat Soup with a Knife: Counterinsurgency Lessons from Malaya and Vietnam*, Chicago, Ill.: University of Chicago Press, 2005.

*National Security Strategy of the United States of America*, Washington, D.C.: White House, March 2006.

Norton, Michael A., *Operational Leadership in Vietnam: General William Depuy vs. Lieutenant General Victor Krulak or Attrition Vice Pacification*, Newport, R.I.: Naval War College, May 19, 1997.

Ollivant, Douglas A., and Eric D. Chewning, "Producing Victory: Rethinking Conventional Forces in COIN Operations," *Military Review*, July–August 2006, pp. 50–59.

Olonisakin, Funmi, *Peacekeeping in Sierra Leone: The Story of UNAMSIL*, Boulder, Colo.: Lynne Rienner Publishers, 2008.

Paul, Christopher, *Information Operations—Doctrine and Practice: A Handbook*, Westport, Conn.: Praeger Security International, 2008.

———, "How Do Terrorists Generate and Maintain Support?" in Paul K. Davis and Kim Cragin, eds., *Social Science for Counterterrorism: Putting the Pieces Together*, Santa Monica, Calif.: RAND Corporation, MG-849-OSD, 2009, pp. 113–150. As of March 2, 2010:
http://www.rand.org/pubs/monographs/MG849/

———, "As a Fish Swims in the Sea: Relationships Between Factors Contributing to Support for Terrorist or Insurgent Groups," *Studies in Conflict and Terrorism*, Vol. 33, No. 6, 2010, pp. 448–510.

Paul, Christopher, Colin P. Clarke, and Beth Grill, *Victory Has a Thousand Fathers: Detailed Counterinsurgency Case Studies*, Santa Monica, Calif.: RAND Corporation, MG-964/1-OSD, 2010. As of June 2010:
http://www.rand.org/pubs/monographs/MG964.1/

Paul, Christopher, Russell W. Glenn, Beth Grill, Megan P. McKernan, Barbara Raymond, Matt Stafford, and Horacio R. Trujillo, "Identifying Urban Flashpoints: A Delphi Derived Model for Scoring Cities' Vulnerability to Large-Scale Unrest," *Studies in Conflict and Terrorism*, Vol. 31, No. 11, 2008, pp. 981–1000.

Pearson, Egon S., and Jerzy Neyman, "On the Problem of Two Samples," in Jerzy Neyman and Egon S. Pearson, *Joint Statistical Papers*, Cambridge, UK: Cambridge University Press, [1930] 1967, pp. 99–115.

Petraeus, David H., "Learning Counterinsurgency: Observations from Soldiering in Iraq," *Military Review*, January–February 2006, pp. 2–12.

Quinlivan, James T., "Force Requirements in Stability Operations," *Parameters*, Winter 1995, pp. 59–69.

Ragin, Charles C., *The Comparative Method: Moving Beyond Qualitative and Quantitative Strategies*, Berkeley, Calif.: University of California Press, 1987.

———, *Fuzzy-Set Social Science*, Chicago, Ill.: University of Chicago Press, 2000.

———, *User's Guide to Fuzzy-Set/Qualitative Comparative Analysis 2.0*, Tucson, Ariz.: Department of Sociology, University of Arizona, 2006.

Ragin, Charles C., Kriss A. Drass, and Sean Davey, *Fuzzy-Set/Qualitative Comparative Analysis 2.0*, Tucson, Ariz.: Department of Sociology, University of Arizona, 2006.

Rosenau, William, "Subversion and Terrorism: Understanding and Countering the Threat," in *The MIPT Terrorism Annual 2006*, Oklahoma City, Okla.: National Memorial Institute for the Prevention of Terrorism, 2006, pp. 53–69.

"Rumsfeld: U.S. Must Drain the Swamp," CNN.com, September 19, 2001. As of October 14, 2009:
http://edition.cnn.com/2001/US/09/18/ret.defense.rumsfeld/index.html

Sepp, Kalev I., "Best Practices in Counterinsurgency," *Military Review*, May–June 2005, pp. 8–12.

*Small Wars Journal* Blog, various dates. As of March 2, 2010: http://smallwarsjournal.com/blog/

Staniland, Paul, "Defeating Transnational Insurgencies: The Best Offense Is a Good Fence," *Washington Quarterly*, Vol. 29, No. 1, Winter 2005–2006, pp. 21–40.

Strategic Communication and Public Diplomacy Policy Coordinating Committee, *U.S. National Strategy for Public Diplomacy and Strategic Communication*, Washington, D.C., 2007. As of March 2, 2010: http://www.cfr.org/publication/13601/

Stryker, Robin, "Beyond History Versus Theory: Strategic Narrative and Sociological Explanation," *Sociological Methods and Research*, Vol. 24, No. 3, 1996, pp. 304–352.

Sun Tzu, *The Art of War*, Lionel Giles, trans., Mineola, N.Y.: Dover, 2002.

U.S. Department of State, *Counterinsurgency for U.S. Government Policymakers: A Work in Progress*, Washington, D.C., October 2007.

U.S. Joint Chiefs of Staff, *Dictionary of Military and Associated Terms*, Joint Publication 1-02, April 21, 2001, as amended through October 31, 2009.

Vinci, Anthony, "The 'Problems of Mobilization' and the Analysis of Armed Groups," *Parameters*, Spring 2006, pp. 49–62.

Vo Nguyen Giap, *People's War People's Army: The Vietcong Insurrection Manual for Underdeveloped Countries*, New York: Praeger, 1962.

Weber, Max, "Politics as a Vocation," in H. H. Gerth and C. Wright Mills, eds., *From Max Weber: Essays in Sociology*, New York: Oxford University Press, 1958.

Weinstein, Jeremy, and Macartan Humphreys, *Disentangling the Determinants of Successful Demobilization and Reintegration*, Working Paper No. 69, Washington, D.C.: Center for Global Development, 2005.

Willis, Thomas E. II, "Lessons from the Past: Successful British Counterinsurgency Operations in Malaya 1948–1960," *Infantry Magazine*, July–August 2005.

SUPPLEMENTAL MATERIAL

# Matrix of Factors Representing 20 Approaches to COIN and Scorecard of Good Versus Bad COIN Practices and Factors

## Matrix of Factors Representing 20 Approaches to COIN

| Factor | | Short-term investments, Improvements in infrastructure/development, or property reform in area of conflict controlled or claimed by COIN force | In area of conflict, COIN force *not* perceived as worse than insurgents | Perception of security created or maintained among population in areas COIN force claimed to control | COIN force established and then expanded secure areas | Government corruption reduced/good governance increased since onset of conflict | COIN force provided or ensured provision of basic services in areas it controlled or claimed to control | Government leaders selected in a manner considered just and fair by majority of population in area of conflict | Majority of citizens in area of conflict viewed government as legitimate | COIN force *not* viewed as an occupying force in area of conflict | Government provided better governance than insurgents in area of conflict | COIN force avoided excessive collateral damage, disproportionate use of … |
|---|---|---|---|---|---|---|---|---|---|---|---|---|
| Development | + | | | | | | | | | | | |
| Pacification | + | | | | | | | | | | | |
| Legitimacy | +/o | | | | | | | | | | | |
| Democracy | o | | | | | | | | | | | |
| Resettlement | – | | | | | | | | | | | |
| Cost-benefit | + | | | | | | | | | | | |
| Border control | + | | | | | | | | | | | |
| "Crush them" | – | | | | | | | | | | | |
| Amnesty/rewards | x | | | | | | | | | | | |
| Strategic communication | + | | | | | | | | | | | |
| COIN FM | + | | | | | | | | | | | |
| "Beat cop" | + | | | | | | | | | | | |
| "Boots on the ground" | + | | | | | | | | | | | |
| "Put a local face on it" | x | | | | | | | | | | | |
| Cultural awareness | x | | | | | | | | | | | |
| Tangible support reduction | + | | | | | | | | | | | |
| Criticality of intelligence | + | | | | | | | | | | | |
| Flexibility and adaptability | + | | | | | | | | | | | |
| Insurgent support strategies | – | | | | | | | | | | | |
| Continuation and contestation | + | | | | | | | | | | | |

**Degree of evidentiary support**

+ = strong support
o = some support
– = strong evidence against
x = cannot be tested